Where Is the Teacher?

Kids today can learn more from a five-minute YouTube Video or AI chatbot than they can from a full day of lectures. So what then is our role as classroom teachers?

In this groundbreaking book, seasoned educator Kyle Wagner explains the new role of the teacher in the 4th industrial revolution. You will learn how to shift from being a deliverer of content, to a thoughtful designer and facilitator of student-centered learning experiences who gently guides from behind the scenes. Kyle, a veteran co-learning experience designer, former classroom teacher, and school leader, unpacks each of the 12 shifts required to build these student-centered environments. Chapters cover how to shift from a content-based to inquiry-based approach; develop relevant, interdisciplinary skills; cultivate meaningful student reflection; curate beautiful, real-world work; facilitate student-led discussion; and more.

Through stories from real student-centered classrooms around each shift, and anecdotes from the author's experience teaching and leading micro-academies, you will come away ready to unleash student creativity, build thoughtful inquirers, and develop self-directed learners within your own context.

Kyle Wagner is the founder and lead PBL/Learning Design Coach for Transform Educational Consulting Limited, an organization that empowers forward thinking schools and educators to create more globally, socially, and emotionally aware citizens through project-based experiences and student-centered environments. Kyle is also the former Coordinator of Futures Academy at the International School of Beijing, has 12 years classroom teaching experience, and worked as a Humanities Teacher at world-renowned High Tech High. He has authored *The Power of SIMPLE*, hosts a popular podcast, and holds an M.Ed. in Teacher Leadership.

Also Available from Routledge Eye On Education

(www.routledge.com/k-12)

Reinventing the Classroom Experience: Learning Anywhere,
Anytime
Nancy Sulla

Students Taking Charge in Grades 6–12: Inside the Learner-
Active, Technology-Infused Classroom
Nancy Sulla

Students Taking Charge in Grades K-5: Inside the Learner-
Active, Technology-Infused Classroom
Nancy Sulla

Passionate Learners, 3rd Edition: How to Engage and Empower
Your Students
Pernille Ripp

What Great Teachers Do Differently, 3rd Edition: Nineteen
Things That Matter Most
Todd Whitaker

Where Is the Teacher?
The 12 Shifts for Student-Centered Environments

Kyle Wagner

Routledge
Taylor & Francis Group

NEW YORK AND LONDON

Designed cover image: © Getty Images

First published 2025
by Routledge
605 Third Avenue, New York, NY 10158

and by Routledge
4 Park Square, Milton Park, Abingdon, Oxon, OX14 4RN

Routledge is an imprint of the Taylor & Francis Group, an informa business

Library of Congress Cataloging-in-Publication Data
Names: Wagner, Kyle, author.
Title: Where is the teacher? : the 12 shifts for student-centered environments / Kyle Wagner.
Description: New York, NY : Routledge, 2024. | Includes bibliographical references.
Identifiers: LCCN 2024006869 (print) | LCCN 2024006870 (ebook) | ISBN 9781032503707 (hardback) | ISBN 9781032484716 (paperback) | ISBN 9781003398226 (ebook)
Subjects: LCSH: Student-centered learning. | Inquiry-based learning. | Teacher effectiveness.
Classification: LCC LB1027.23 .W27 2024 (print) | LCC LB1027.23 (ebook) | DDC 378.1/794--dc23/eng/20240214
LC record available at https://lccn.loc.gov/2024006869
LC ebook record available at https://lccn.loc.gov/2024006870

ISBN: 978-1-032-50370-7 (hbk)
ISBN: 978-1-032-48471-6 (pbk)
ISBN: 978-1-003-39822-6 (ebk)

DOI: 10.4324/9781003398226

Typeset in Palatino
by SPi Technologies India Pvt Ltd (Straive)

*For my life mentors, Daniel Bauer and Rob Riordan.
You have lit a pathway to Ednovation I never knew existed.*

*For Mom. You taught me that nothing is impossible
once you get started.*

Contents

Acknowledgments

I never intended to write a book. I simply wanted to find the best way to share inspiring stories of classroom transformation.

Three years ago, I embarked on a journey to find those stories. It was 2021, and the world was enveloped by COVID, forcing educators to teach in environments they had never before experienced. Many decided to leave the profession, with good reason. But another story began to unfold as well. Some courageous educators used this changing landscape as an invitation to re-design how learning was delivered. Through new technological mediums, project-based experiences, and personalized pathways, they began empowering learners to take charge of their own learning.

I discovered these stories via a growing LinkedIn Community; we were eager to rewrite the narrative for how we school kids. I started a podcast, authored blog posts, and wrote weekly newsletters to share these stories with a wider community around how they too could take steps into student-centered environments.

This book is a culmination of three years of stories and the impact they had on kids, from educators of all walks of life who transformed from deliverers of content to facilitators of learning.

My biggest thank you goes to them. Thank you to the 50+ educators who were willing to be vulnerable; take risks in the classroom, and share your journey with a wider community, so they could make the shifts as well. Thank you for your honesty around both your triumphs and challenges.

Stories benefit from a powerful narrative, and the shifting landscape of education has certainly provided it. But they benefit even more when they can center around a simple and repeatable framework for teaching and learning. Thank you to my life mentor and greatest hero, Rob Riordan, for providing the seed for that framework. That folded piece of paper you handed me

20 years ago outlining shifts in practice when I first welcomed students into my classroom at High Tech High has become my manifesto. It has provided direction for countless others.

Thank you to my other life mentor and "chief ruckus maker" Daniel Bauer for helping resurrect and expand upon that framework, develop a simple scorecard for educators to evaluate practice through it, and focus all of my energy around how to help educators realize it in their classrooms.

Thank you to my first tribe of EDNOVATORS! Thank you for sacrificing 90 minutes every week to nerd out about learning and kids. Thank you for your willingness to discuss the shifts and the ensuing impact they were making in your classroom, from pre-K through high school: Rosie, Trevett, Maria, Yang, Matt— you know who you are.

Thank you to the 20+ schools and educational leaders willing to pilot the student-centered shifts and put them in their teachers' hands. There are too many of you to name, but I want to acknowledge Betzy Orenos, Sheila Escobedo, Mari Simpson, Natalie Harvey, and Anne Robinson for having the unparalleled vision to see the potential of student-centered learning within every teacher's classroom, regardless of subject, age, or years of teaching experience.

Thank you Lauren Davis and the Routledge Eye for Education team. You believed in me and my story before I even put a word on the page. Thank you for convincing me that this book could be more than just another guide for developing project-based experiences, but instead, a framework for how all learning could be delivered. Your global footprint and willingness to disseminate this with a wider community has affirmed that we have a message that resonates.

Thank you Deborah McNally and Claire Peet for providing feedback and ensuring the narrative of transformation shared as much of the challenges as it did the triumphs. Somehow between steering professional development and instructional practice for one of the largest networks of schools in Asia, you managed to provide timely feedback. It is a testament to the kind of people you are.

Thank you to my mom. Despite suffering a severe head injury that robbed you of your ability to read, you managed to write a book far superior to mine. You taught me that achieving anything comes from building habits and finishing what you start.

Thank you to the titans of student-centered practices who first lit a path for us pioneers. John Dewey, Jean Piaget, Paulo Friere, and Maria Montessori—you were authors, scientists, and anthropologists in addition to being revolutionary teachers. Thank you for being eons ahead of your time.

Finally, thank you to the countless student-centered practitioners whose stories aren't featured in the book. By showing up every day, elevating your student's voices, and co-designing learning experiences and environments with them, you are building a brighter tomorrow.

Meet the Author

 **Kyle Wagner** is the founder and lead PBL/ Learning Design Coach for Transform Educational Consulting Limited, an organization that empowers forward-thinking schools and educators to create more globally, socially, and emotionally aware citizens through project-based experiences and student-centered environments. He has trained educators in schools around the world to develop transformative learning experiences for their students, and the student-centered environments to support them. Kyle is also the former Coordinator of Futures Academy at the International School of Beijing, has 12 years classroom teaching experience, and worked as a Humanities Teacher at world-renowned High Tech High. He has authored *The Power of SIMPLE*, hosts a popular podcast, and holds an M.Ed. in Teacher Leadership focused on developing student-centered classrooms and distributed leadership models.

Introduction

The Wizard of Learner-Centered Environments Pulls Back the Curtains

I will never forget first stepping foot in High Tech High that sunny Monday morning. It was more X- men Xavier institute than it was school. When I opened the double glass doors, there weren't your standard big oak desks and formal receptionists who managed the front office. Instead, there were two prepubescent teenagers, in buttoned up, plaid collar shirts.

'Hi, you must be Kyle.'

I coughed.

"Well, usually people call me Mr. Wagner, but you can call me Mr. Kyle if you want."

"Sure, Mr. Kyle. Welcome to High Tech High."

My eyes had to register what I was taking in.

Here were two students, no older than 12 or 13, greeting me with more warmth than grown adults would in the same position.

But that wasn't what shocked me the most.

Behind these poised students was a room that resembled more a summer camp than a school.

The large open space was filled with students who were actively tinkering, discussing, exploring, building, writing, and I must assume "learning." Two excitable boys were busy fastening a rope around a cylinder shaped stone, and attaching it to a wood ramp. Within earshot, three girls sat facing each other, deep in conversation. As a middle school teacher, I assumed it had to be around the latest teen gossip or social media memes. But when I moved closer, I heard them mention phrases like "fostering social justice" and "ideas for building more just laws."

In another corner of the room, three students sat cross-legged on the floor, captivated by an older peer who flipped gracefully

DOI: 10.4324/9781003398226-1

through note cards and uttered phrases like "What I learned through this project" and, "How I have grown as a learner."

I blinked a few times to make sure I wasn't dreaming.

This is the kind of learning environment you hope to create for maybe one day a year.

But at High Tech High, this was the norm.

I, unfortunately, wasn't ready for it.

I immediately put on my "teacher hat."

"What are you building?" I asked the two boys with the stone cylinder and rope.

Without looking up, they proclaimed in unison, "A simple machine."

My proverbial teacher hat was now fully fastened around my forehead.

"For what?"

At this point I was clearly a distraction. After the rope was in place, they wrapped it around the edge of the ramp and began dragging it up the slope.

Their eyes bulged and one shouted, "It works!"

At that moment, an adult in loosely fit jeans, with a carefully groomed beard and wavy hair not unlike a surfer in a vintage film, emerged from the nearby classroom.

He high-fived each student in shared jubilation. "Great job! What did you learn?"

"We figured out how the Egyptians did it. We understand how they built the pyramids!"

Later I learned that every student in that space was working on the same *big* question but answering it in their own creative way. The girls in the corner were exploring advancements in law and social justice for Ancient Egyptian women and slaves, in order to write their own "code of ethics." The boys with the ramp were exploring advancements in technology and building a simple machine to demonstrate how Ancient Egyptians created one of history's greatest marvels. The boy presenting in the middle was reflecting on what he learned from writing and publishing his first book of Egyptian myths written for the modern era.

The Big Question they were all answering: How can we communicate the contributions of the Ancient Egyptians to modern society through a living museum?

This was high-quality project-based learning at the Mecca of best practice.

But this story is not about project-based learning, nor High Tech High.

It's about what happens when we put learners at the center of their learning journeys.

Creating the kind of magic I witnessed that day doesn't come from one or two teacher "tricks."

It comes from continual trial and error, reflection, and a deep-seated belief that learners are capable of charting their own paths.

I told you earlier that I wasn't ready for High Tech High. I wasn't lying.

That day I described was part of a "bonanza" hiring process that began at 7 AM and wouldn't finish until half past five. I would deliver a lesson; sit through interviews conducted by students and staff; co-design a project with a team of teacher practitioners; and chat informally with current teachers about my teaching philosophy.

But I wasn't ready to be interviewed by 12- and 13-year-old kids or be called by my first name.

Or watch as they scrutinized my lesson plan for how it could have better fit their needs.

I wasn't ready to partner with other subject teachers and co-design a learning experience in less than 30 minutes.

I wasn't ready to be asked what I thought I did "well" and where I could improve.

I was just a third-year humanities teacher, who was pretty damn good with a class of students seated nicely in rows, but out of place with a class full of learners who were able to choose their own pathways.

How about you? Are you ready for "learner-centered environments"?

Because it requires us to abandon nearly everything we learned in formal teacher training.

It means instead of …

1. Designing learning experiences in a silo - - - -> We co-design with our learners
2. Leading learning with content - - - -> We lead with inquiry
3. Designing learning around teacher questions - - - -> We design experiences around student questions
4. Viewing our subject as a body of knowledge - - - -> We view subject(s) as a lens to see the world
5. Asking students to fill in worksheets - - - -> We let them build a product/service that serves a purpose in the real world
6. Evaluating our students with grades - - - -> We motivate our students through pursuit of their interests
7. Measuring learning outcomes by products - - - -> We reflect continuously on the learning process
8. Creating a competitive environment - - - -> We build a collaborative culture for task completion
9. Delivering lectures - - - -> We facilitate Socratic discussion and dialogue
10. Monitoring progress on our own - - - -> We entrust students, peers, and experts to provide feedback and critique
11. Organizing class presentations - - - -> We commission authentic, public audiences for student work
12. Learning from a textbook and academia - - - -> We partner with the community

We can't begin to embody these 12 shifts after a half-day PD in an overcrowded auditorium.

We can embody them only after years of commitment to designing learning experiences around our students.

But this is not completely new territory for us.

You probably already do a few of these things well.

Perhaps you have set up stations in your classroom when learning new material and have empowered students to manage them.

Perhaps you have set up a workshop-like environment with short mini-lessons on various topics and conference regularly with students according to their needs.

Bravo.

The truth is, none of us, even the most skilled practitioners, have mastered the 12 key shifts for learner-centered environments.

Where did the 12 shifts come from?

Remember how I told you I wasn't ready for the magic that was High Tech High?

I wasn't ready, but I was persistent.

After not getting hired the first go around, I spent the next year improving my craft at my current school, 30 miles away.

I started allowing students to choose alternative pathways to the prescribed curriculum.

Put on self-directed plays around history principles I was required to teach.

Constructed models of the ancient cities we explored.

It wasn't 100 percent learner-centered; it wasn't even "project-based"; but it was a step in the right direction.

And the hiring team at High Tech High took notice.

Following the second "bonanza," I was given the keys to my first wall-to-wall project-based, learner-centered classroom at High Tech High.

Along with the keys, the co-founder of High Tech High handed me a single sheet of paper that made absolutely no sense at the time.

It listed nine characteristics of student-centered classrooms with arrows going one or two ways.

Each characteristic was intended as a guidepost for the kind of classroom High Tech High hoped I would create.

The first few months, I can almost guarantee that they observed nothing of what they were looking for. I was too overwhelmed with the responsibility of designing a curriculum and deep, meaningful learning experiences from scratch.

But over time, with coaching and support from my beloved mentor and co-founder of High Tech High, Rob Riordan, I began to make each shift. And my students soared because of it.

They mentored each other in areas where they required support.

Sought out community partners for projects and questions they wished to explore.

Assessed their own learning and set their own goals and deadlines for development.

I shifted from being a teacher to a facilitator who coached, supported, and inquired from the sidelines.

I treated my 11–12-year-old students the same way I would an adult; and they did adult work because of it.

They acted as museum curators to curate their own living museums of the civilizations we studied.

Acted as authors to publish e-books around cultural identity.

As business owners, to manage their own social enterprises to serve the community.

Those nine characteristics of learner-centered environments later evolved into 12 key shifts that would transform my classroom forever.

Making these 12 shifts will also transform learning in yours.

But the purpose of this book is not to share my story of transformation.

It's to share the stories of countless educators *just* like you, who have used the 12 shifts to transform learning in theirs, and simple ways to integrate the shifts within your own classroom context.

It's the story of how Rosie Westwall used the co-creation shift to empower her five-year-old learners to organize weekly climate strikes.

The story of how Brett Carrier used the self-management shift to transform her Year 5 humanities students into local food truck owners.

The story of how Linda Amici used the student inquiry shift to help Year 3 students enact citizen science projects with local universities around "cleaning up Westerville."

The story of how Kristin Damburger used the Peer-to-Peer Collaboration shift to transform her Year 8 science students into space colonists and physicists.

The story of how Michele Willis used the Authentic, Public Audience shift to reshape her passive Year 10 humanities students into active podcast producers who shared untold stories from the community.

What transformation story will you tell? Your story of transformation goes here: _____.

Making these shifts doesn't require the perfect conditions.

They are as much for the public school teacher who teaches six classes a day as they are for the homeschool pod leader who gathers students twice a week.

But they do require us to think differently.

We must no longer think of ourselves as teachers—but rather as learning *experience* designers.

In the same way that water flows freely from the mountain to the sea, our job is to design the conditions that allow our students to manage and direct their own learning.

Each chapter in this book is designed to help you do that.

They include an overview of each shift; stories from real practitioners around what it looks like in action; and commonsense tips for how to apply the shifts in your own learning environment.

Stories come from learner-centered environments all over the world.

As a young 25-year-old, I thought High Tech High was the most innovative place on earth; now I know that this kind of innovation is happening everywhere.

In remote jungles of Indonesia, where students are powering schoolbuses with unused cooking oil, to large thousand-plus urban campuses in Australia, where students are running their own electives.

Warning This book is not a "how-to" guide.

We've got way too many of those.

Rather, it is a manifesto to help you develop the *mindset* required to let go and some practical tools and ways to get started.

Before we get started, I want to start with an exercise I use with all of my adult pupils.

I want you to close your eyes. Imagine you have just stepped foot in a classroom, school, or learning space completely *owned* by students.

What are they doing? How are they working? If you could amplify their conversations, what kind of things would you hear them discussing?

Next, try to find the teacher (or "learning experience designer.") What are they doing?

Finally, draw or find a picture that represents the visual you just constructed in your mind. It can be of your current learning environment or one you have seen enacted elsewhere. Place it in the box provided. Over the next 12 chapters, we are going to create it.

Vision for your Classroom...

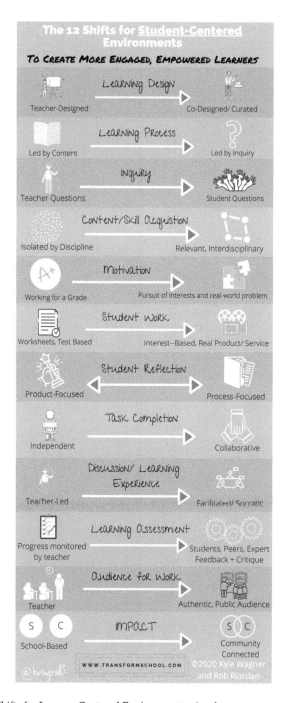

IMAGE 0.1 Shifts for Learner-Centered Environments visual

Part I

Learner-Centered Design and Unleashing Student Inquiry

1

Shift #1: From Teacher-Designed Learning to Co-designed Learning

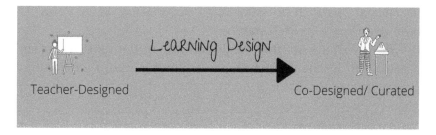

IMAGE 1.1 Shift 1 Learning Design Shift

> And they all developed a project themselves that they wanted to do and they had to create some sort of product and end show. And that was incredibly powerful because I had these kids that I just couldn't engage all year. No matter what I did, I could not engage these kids. And suddenly they were coming in during lunch to work on their projects.
>
> —Luna Rey

Luna Rey had tried every trick in the book, and none of it was working.

DOI: 10.4324/9781003398226-3

She tried enlivening her dry English curriculum through workshops and discussion, but her classroom was often eerily silent.

She tried having students learn about historical narratives through writing about the recent level 5 hurricane that ravaged through their city, but students didn't want to put any words on the page.

She tried animating the scripted curriculum she was given by developing hands-on activities, but students refused to participate.

> I just started teaching the exact way they wanted me to teach. And I really hated it. It honestly was soul sucking because I felt like I wasn't passionate about it.
>
> –Luna Rey

Luna's school wrongfully assumed that because Luna was a new teacher, she needed pre-developed materials, tests, and curriculum to ensure a smooth start.

But by doing so, they neglected one of the most important lessons of learner-centered environments—your curriculum walks through your door every day. Students carry with them their own stories, narratives, lessons, insights, and expertise. It's our responsibility to uncover them.

It's not as if this concept was foreign to Luna. After all, she spent much of her own childhood learning at a Waldorf School, Museum School, and High Tech High, developing her passions and interests through projects that were personally meaningful to her.

But somehow, as a teacher in her current Title I, underperforming school, learning was supposed to look different. The most important mandate was that students "catch up."

After trying one failed intervention after another, Luna had an epiphany.

> The reality is not every kid is going to go get a PhD. So we need to prepare students for whatever they're passionate about and help them understand how to interact with others, how to present their ideas, how to be passionate

about different things, and be intrinsically motivated to get through the hard times.

—Luna Rey

Luna tried something radically different.

She ditched the mandated, scripted curriculum and pacing guides, and asked students what *they* wanted to learn.

Their only mandate was to pursue a question they found personally meaningful and develop a project to help answer it.

And like a light switch being flicked on for the very first time, her classroom came alive.

One team of students transformed into capable engineers, fixing broken desks, chairs, and internal components of computers. A pair of students became the class programmers, helping classmates develop personal websites and create animated games. One extroverted girl became the Instagram influencer, teaching others how to harness the power of social media to build a brand and positively influence popular culture.

And that was incredibly powerful because I had these kids that I just couldn't engage with all year. No matter what I did, I could not engage these kids. And they were coming in during lunch to work on their projects.

—Luna Rey

Luna's experience is not unlike ours.

We all have students who possess their own unique interests, strengths, and ideas. As student-centered practitioners, it is our job to co-design experiences that harness them.

Co-creation means that rather than molding our students to our curriculum, we mold our curriculum to them.

I know what you might be thinking. I've got a packed curriculum to teach, standards to cover, and material to test. And that probably is true. Co-creation doesn't require us to start completely from scratch. We can invite our students into the same planning process we undergo in designing learning experiences around our curriculum.

Linda Amici, a student-centered educator in Westerville, Ohio, harnessed the power of co-creation by inviting her Year 5 students to plan around what she described as her "most hated academic standards": Ancient Western civilizations. Linda didn't feel energized by these standards mainly because they didn't stick. Her students would memorize the information for the assessment, and then quickly move on to other, more relevant learning. As Linda recalls, "They had nothing to do with their own lives."

But with a slight re-frame, suddenly they did.

Her class co-created a big question to give these standards new meaning: "What can we learn from the successes and failures of early civilizations of the Western Hemisphere that we can apply to our lives today?"

Suddenly learning was purposeful, and her class sprung to life as a result.

Students interested in food and cuisine researched the modest diet of Ancient Mayans, and after learning of their ability to self-sustain, developed a recipe book for how to create healthier meals today. Students interested in architecture explored the infrastructure of Machu Picchu, and after learning about its overall layout, developed architectural plans for modern-day buildings. Students interested in technology and warfare researched the border conflicts faced by the Aztecs, and after learning about their eventual demise, suggested laws that would better protect our borders today.

Linda's students dove deeper into her curriculum than she ever could have hoped for if designing these learning experiences in isolation.

As Linda recalls, "All of these projects can be connected to the different standards. When you make [learning] something that is relevant to them, they remember it too."

Linda's role as teacher shifted from delivering these standards from the front of the classroom to seeking evidence of student learning in each of their projects by coaching on the side. When students explored the territory of each civilization in order to learn how to better protect modern-day borders, Linda checked off her geography standards. When students looked at primary-source documents of ancient laws and government procedure in order to write their own code of ethics, Linda checked off her government standards.

What are your most hated standards? How could taking a "co-creation" approach help you bring them to life?

Co-creation with the Community

Co-creation requires us to invite more than just our learners into the planning process.

Jill Clayton, a seasoned learner-centered practitioner, begins the design of many of her learning experiences by partnering with the community. She develops relationships with businesses, parks, and organizations that surround her school and explores ways in which her students might serve them.

When she learned that the local golf courses around her school needed to better understand the birds that inhabited their space, she invited students to conduct the study by constructing birdhouses to track migratory patterns. Students partnered with the Audubon Society to design the birdhouses and place them in the trees that lined each fairway. They presented their findings to the golf course board to inform course design. In the same way Linda integrated her most hated Civilization standards, Jill was able to integrate her most dreaded math and science standards at appropriate times within the learning experience.

We often begrudge math as being impossibly tough to co-design learning experiences around.

But in another spark of co-creation, Jill partnered her students with their local ski resort to study slope through avalanche monitoring and testing.

And finally, to delve deeper into Earth science, Jill partnered with the local Starbucks to have students construct and fill planter boxes with seasonal plants for their outdoor space.

Through each instance of co-creation, Jill saw herself less as a teacher and more as an "entrepreneur, who looks at what is around [her] and kind of figures it out."

As a teacher entrepreneur, what opportunities for co-creation exist within your community?

To help you answer this question, we are going to take a trip to a 100 percent student-centered school situated in the heart of urban Philadelphia. The Revolution School lives and breathes by a simple motto: "A place where students co-create their unique academic journey." As the lead teacher entrepreneur, Dr. Jane Shore knows her job is not to devise learning experiences in a siloed classroom or private office, but to build them organically in partnership with students, educators, and key stakeholders in the community.

Revolution School students partnered with a local urban farm to lead meditation and healing sessions. Formed bonds with the shelter across the street to cook and prepare organic meals for the homeless.

Connected with the local minority-owned golf course to teach disadvantaged pupils math and literacy concepts through sport.

Dr. Jane understands the importance of learning co-ownership. When building learning partners, it's not just a classroom full of students invested in the success of learning experiences, but an entire community.

So where's the starting point for these learning experiences?

Before any project is built, students first begin by co-constructing a community map. Equipped with clipboards, a pencil, and their own creativity, students take a walk around the community and map out key landmarks (See Image 1.2).

After devising the maps, students decide on the places where they might build deeper connections. They reach out via email, phone, or sometimes in a face-to-face visit that begins with a gentle knock on the door. Together, students and the community partner explore possibilities for collaboration.

Sometimes, the collaboration is simply an extension of an existing project or service the organization already offers, like the wellness classes that were offered every weekend in the local park. As a teacher entrepreneur, Jane's job is simply to seek connections that align to student interests and apply what students are already learning as part of the curriculum.

IMAGE 1.2 Student-Drawn Community Map of Philadelphia

With the urban farm, it was Earth science and social-emotional wellness.

With the local shelter, it was food science and humanities.

With the local golf course tutoring program, math and literacy.

If you are feeling intimidated by such an open approach to community co-creation, you might start by mapping around a pre-determined theme, key stakeholder, or big question. This is the approach learner-centered facilitator Alfie Chung took in Hong Kong when helping middle school students at a local international school devise their maps. Some students mapped the community according to the theme of accessibility; others, from the point of view of tourists; and even more, as local families. Mapping according to each of these unique themes and perspectives provided a key starting point for projects or learning experiences that might be borne in partnership with the community.

IMAGE 1.3 Student-Created Community Problems Map

KEY QUESTIONS FOR REFLECTION

What organizations, landmarks, and businesses exist in your community?

What are some of their existing projects, outreaches, or services they provide? How might you connect your curriculum and learners to these existing experiences?

The Space Podcast: Co-design in a Simple Three-Column Chart

Admittedly, co-design can be a lengthy process. It requires us as educators to take a step back from our mandated curriculum and, first, listen to the interests, ideas, and wonderings of our learners. But in a system where there is so much content to cover, how do we find time to allow for co-creation?

Sara Lev, one of the leading voices on learner-centered environments and experiences in early childhood, faced this same dilemma when her four-to-five-year-olds moved to online learning during the pandemic. Suddenly she would have even less face-to-face time with learners yet with the same requirements of curriculum coverage. But Sara didn't panic. Instead, she took the same approach she would in a learner-centered classroom; she started with simple provocations.

In short, 20-minute virtual home visits, Sara had each learner show her anything they found significant in their home. Some showed their favorite toys, while others described the different corners of their bedrooms. As learners navigated through each room, Sara jotted down observations around what she saw. She was hoping to better understand their interests and how it might connect to topics within her curriculum. After 20 engaging walk-throughs, she made a startling discovery. Many learners had a fascination with *outer space*.

Some learners had pillow cases shaped as planets.

Others had telescopes to observe faraway stars.

Some had miniature planets and glow-in-the-dark stars that hung from the ceiling.

Others had NASA posters and T-shirts, space bedsheets, LEGO rocket ships, even a telescope!

The spark for her next learning experience was instantaneously born. Students would explore the vast expanse of space. But from what lens? That answer came serendipitously in a suggestion from the PBL Facebook Group Sara manages.

How about a podcast?

The suggestion was perfect. Sara's husband was busy recording another episode of his podcast, "Meeting Tom Cruise," a podcast that features hilarious celebrity encounters with the peculiar star in order to give a glimpse of what he is like in real life.

Sara's brain went to work: *What if students created a podcast exploring the vast mysteries of space?*

After launching the idea of a podcast a few weeks later, her learners were over the moon with excitement.

Here's where the "facilitator of learning experiences" part comes in …

Sara had never created a podcast, taught for an extended period of time online, or co-created in a remote space. But she *trusted* her learners—and they built the experience together. They decided together which topics they would cover, the stories they would write, the interviews they would conduct, and the episodes they would produce. And students brought ideas Sara might never have thought of if designing completely on her own. With the help of his mom, one child helped secure an interview with her colleague at SpaceX; one child built a "space set" for the podcast out of his bedroom to assist with story creation. As the "facilitator of learning," Sara helped guide the process, developing key milestones, infusing curriculum in relevant places, and assessing learning goals as each target was met.

How might you use this case study as inspiration for the learning experiences you co-design? What observations have you made about your students and their interests? How might these observations connect to the mandated curriculum?

The Simple Co-design Chart

Do you have a free whiteboard wall in your room? It's time to put it to good use in partnership with your learners. First, divide it into three equal columns using masking tape (preferably colored). On the top of Column #1, write the heading "Curricular Topics"; above Column #2, "Student Interests"; above Column #3, "Authentic Project/Learning Experience Ideas." Beginning with column #1, equipped with your curriculum in hand, list the topics that emerge on separate Post-It notes. If teaching Humanities, topics might include "forms of government" or "characteristics of ancient civilizations"; if teaching science, topics might include "evolution" or "genetics." After brainstorming at least ten topics, supply your students with Post-It notes and ask them to write down their interests. This might include "playing music," "space Exploration," or even "making YouTube videos." Have them place the Post-Its in column #2 and add your own Post-Its based on observations you have made based on conversations you have overheard, games/activities you have seen them involved in, or conversations you have had with their parents. After accumulating all of the Post-Its, group them into similar categories. For example, if one student listed "drumming," and another "singing," you might create a category around "making music." With these two columns populated, you now have the two main ingredients for co-designing student-centered learning experiences and environments. The final step is to link Column #1 and #2 Post-Its together in a meaningful learning experience.

Below is an example of that co-design chart.

Curricular or Cross-Curricular Topic	Student Interests	Authentic Project/Learning Experience Ideas
Immigration	Minecraft and Metaverse	Building sustainable future civilizations in the Metaverse based on innovations from the past using Minecraft
Ancient Civilizations	Tik Tok	
Government	Making Music	
Economics	Making YouTube Videos	
World Geography	Video Games	
Journalism	Programming	
Short Stories	Discord and Chat Channels	
Poetic Imagery	Vlogs	
Social Justice	Space	How can a student produced podcast help our peers get excited about space?
Plot Structure	Social Media	

This simple co-design chart helped spark a quarter-long entrepreneurship project in a Year 3 classroom in Lahore, Pakistan. On the other side of that same school, it sparked a living museum of Ancient Egypt with student-created pottery, jewelry, hieroglyphs, and other artifacts.

What learning experiences might the three-column spark in your classroom?

The Challenges with Co-design

Let me make one thing abundantly clear: Co-design is not for the novice teacher. If you are brand new to teaching, designing an extended unit of study that includes learning goals, lessons, activities, assessment criteria, big understandings, and a cohesive way to organize student work is already a tall task to achieve. And in the same way we all learned to ride a bike by first putting on training wheels, we must first develop the mindsets for effective learning experience design before we invite full input from our learners. Students also need those training wheels. My first project as a teacher was a "shoebox museum" experience borrowed from the teacher across the street. It was pre-planned, and had all the supplementary resources organized nicely in a digital folder for easy access. Was it effective? Partially. Students had a lot of fun creating their museums and had choice in how they looked! Plus, I was able to cover some important curriculum standards and incorporate student interests in the process. And while it was definitely teacher-centric, it provided the training wheels I needed to feel confident with more open, student-centered co-design.

I imagine it will be the same for you.

Student-centric design runs on a continuum. You might invite learners to co-create expectations, assessment rubrics, or how they will exhibit learning at the end of a unit or project; but design the activities, trips, lessons, and experiments to help deepen their learning along the way.

As you invite learners to make more decisions about their learning, they will feel more confident in co-constructing it with you.

Here are ten ways to co-design learning experiences from easiest to most challenging:

- Create a Google Form/Survey inviting students to provide input on the next unit of study
- Develop provocations and activities that allow you to observe what students are interested in
- Launch units and learning experiences with an activity that invites learner inquiry (more on this in the next Shift)
- Provide a menu of options for students to fulfill project/unit requirements and allow them to choose the one that most appeals to them
- Co-design expectations for Student Work based on models or real-world exemplars
- Conduct morning circle time at least once a week to gather learner feedback and input
- Create collaborative opportunities for learning and allow learners to choose their teams (more on this in Shift #8: "Task Completion")
- Bring in learning experiences/projects from the community and invite learners to co-create with stakeholders
- Ask students what problems/challenges they want to solve, and infuse your curriculum around them
- Use the three-column chart referenced above and co-design your next learning experience using all three

Where Do You Fall on the Co-design Continuum?

Want to find out where you rank on the "teacher-designed" to "co-designed" shift? Take the scorecard below:

Learning Design

	Teacher Designed < -> Co-designed				
	1	2	3	4		
Learning Design	Seedling (Sower)	Budding (Builder)	Blossoming (Beacon)	Flourishing (Facilitator)	NOW	NEXT
	Teacher designs entire learning experience w/ accompanying resources, materials, activities and assessments. Students have no choice or voice in what they research or learn. Schedule is fixed from Day One.	Teacher designs unit with some input from students on resources, materials, activities and assessments. Students still have limited choice and voice in what they research, learn or produced. Schedule is mostly fixed.	Learning Facilitator designs unit with some input from students before launch. Students provide feedback on resources, materials, activities, and assessments but not in the development. Students have choice in products and sub-topics they research or learn. Schedule more open but still with clear restraints.	Learning experience/ project/ or unit of study is co-designed and student driven from start to finish. Students co-design resources, materials, activities and choose how they will be assessed. Students have complete voice and choice in products, and relevant topics they research or learn. Schedule is highly flexible and co-constructed based on constant input from students. Facilitator acts as learning facilitator and co-designer.		

Reflective Questions

1. How might you discover your students' interests, passions, and areas of strength?
2. What provocations might you set up to learn more about your students?
3. Which part of your curriculum might students already have experience with? How might you discover this?
4. Which part of your schedule could you open up?
5. Where might you provide more opportunities for student voice and choice in learning? Learning products? Demonstrations of Learning? How are they assessed?

TEACHER-DESIGN

 TELLS

LINEAR LE

DESIGNED IN ISOLATION

CURRICULAR FOCUSED

ONGOING OUTPUT

SINGLE LEARNING PATHWAY

LIMITED STAKEHOLDERS

TEACHER AS COMMANDER

CU
CH

@kwagssd3
© 2020 Kyle Wagner and Rob Riordan

TRANSFORM
EDUCATIONAL CONSULTING

IMAGE 1.4 Shift 1 Co-design Infographic

CO-DESIGNED CURATED

...NG

ASKS QUESTIONS

...NED WTH STUDENTS

THROUGH COMMITTEES PANE...

MULTIPLE STAKEHOLDERS

MULITPLE LEARNING PATHWAYS

CO-CONSTRUCTED EVALUATION

...LAR+COMMUNITY+ ...TEREST FOCUSED

TEACHER AS OBSERVER

2

Shift #2: From Content-Led Learning to Inquiry-Based Learning

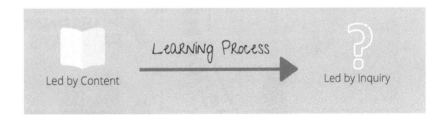

IMAGE 2.1 Shift 2 Learning Process

> Students are completely at the center of the entire school. They are involved in all of the decision-making. They have shared responsibility and use their voice to write the rules of the school. They don't want to wear shoes, they don't have to. So it is about them taking real ownership of their journey and their decision making, and that happens within the curriculum as well.
>
> —Rosie Howes

This story begins seven years ago on a warm day in sunny Southern California. Two dogs played together joyfully, their tails wagging furiously as they chased each other across the

DOI: 10.4324/9781003398226-4

grass. They wrestled and tumbled over each other, barking and yapping in excitement. I smiled as I watched in the large school playground. One of the dogs was my adopted terrier, a strong mother of five, with a white fur coat that browned with only a hint of dust in the air, and the other was my neighbor's gold-endoodle, an energetic three-year-old who could run halfway across the city without tiring. In the enclosed gated area, they both ran freely, safe from the busy street traffic only steps away.

I was on doggy patrol for the weekend. My neighbor, Daisy's (the cute goldendoodle's) owner, had just left that morning for a business trip, and I was entrusted to Daisy's care.

Big mistake.

While I was the laissez-faire pet owner who preferred to keep a dog off leash and trust that she would remain close to my side, my neighbor had a different set of rules.

In the gated area, Daisy was free to run around off leash, but outside of that area, I was given strict instructions to always keep Daisy on the leash.

It was this specific instruction I neglected that almost cost Daisy her life.

Because while I knew better than to unleash Daisy anywhere near the street, I wasn't as cautious when arriving 30 minutes later to a large, unenclosed park with both dogs.

Assuming Daisy would behave in the same manner as Candy in this new environment, I reached down to unhook her from her leash and speak to her eye to eye.

Assuming she spoke English as fluently as Candy, I uttered the following phrase: "Now, Daisy, I am going to let you off of your leash to play, but remember to stay close."

I can't even remember if I finished my sentence.

Because the second I unhooked her, she was gone. And to my horror, she galloped directly toward the busiest traffic in the city. My heart was literally in my throat, and there was no stopping her.

Lottery ticket holders have a greater chance of winning the jackpot than Daisy did of crossing that street unscathed. I closed my eyes as she entered. I couldn't bear to watch.

But to my surprise Daisy made it. And it wasn't just that street crossing where Daisy defied death—she crossed at least half a dozen more before returning to the only home she ever knew. Meanwhile, I thought I had lost Daisy forever.

Thirty minutes later in my desperate search for Daisy my phone lit up with the last person I wanted to hear from: Daisy's owner, Cindy. I answered wondering how I would disclose to her the traumatic news that I had lost her dog.

"Hi, Kyle. I have Daisy here with me. What happened?"

I was floored. Somehow Daisy had navigated her way all the way home and caught Cindy right before she would leave for the airport.

Daisy was safe, and I learned a valuable lesson. Not *all* dogs are ready to be let off the leash.

Why do I tell this story?

Because it is the same reality we face when building student-centered environments.

Not all of our learners are ready to be let off the leash. Our expectation that students manage, develop, direct, prioritize, and map their own learning journeys is a big ask.

They still need us.

Yet as mentioned in the previous shift on co-design, it's not from a teacher who stands in the front of the classroom, but rather one who inquires, probes, and provokes gently from the side.

In this way, learning experiences are guided by inquiry and curiosity, not content.

Similar to co-design, inquiry comes in many forms. Sometimes it's guided by us, and other times it's completely open, and learner- led. According to the Lewis Center for Educational Research, there are three types of inquiry (1):

Structured Inquiry: Learners investigate a teacher-presented question through prescribed procedure, milestones, and activities.

Guided Inquiry: Learners investigate a co-created question through co-designed activities and procedures, milestones, and activities.

Open Inquiry: Learners investigate questions that are student formulated through student designed and selected procedures, milestones, and activities.

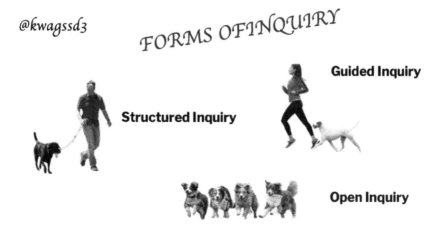

IMAGE 2.2 Three Forms of Inquiry Visual

Of course, as student-centered practitioners, we have as the goal to inspire open inquiry. But I have rarely witnessed it. I observed it once in a Year 5 Montessori classroom where twenty five students moved freely about the classroom, engaged in 25 different activities, accessing resources and completing tasks as if the teacher didn't exist.

For us mere mortals, structured or guided inquiry is far more achievable in the short term. It's the leash that we can continue to lengthen once learners have the tools, strategies, and question-formulating techniques to manage experiences on their own.

The good news is that we can always be the "invisible hand" guiding in the background.

Here's an example.

The Inquiry Process in Action in Project-Based Experiences

One hundred students stood huddled together, trying to keep warm in an abandoned field in Shunyi, Beijing. They had no idea where they were or why they were there.

The only thing they knew was that this learning environment looked far different from the one they were in 30 minutes ago. Thirty minutes earlier they were in their classrooms, jotting down notes from a lecture delivered by their teacher at the front of the classroom. When an all-school fire alarm reverberated across every classroom, they were hurriedly shuffled outside the school, packed onto buses, and taken to this abandoned field.

They now stood, huddled together, staring collectively at large blue tents, occupied by adults in lab coats.

Welcome to the first stage of the inquiry process for the Phoenix Project, a guided inquiry process that would require students to rebuild society after being displaced by an earthquake. In this seven-week learning journey, the responsibility of the teachers (i.e., facilitators) was simply to create the vessel and parameters for the experience and then allow students to fill it.

The large abandoned field was stage #1. After students received food rations, a quick temperature/health check, and an information card providing more details around the simulated disaster, it would be up to them to determine how to rebuild society.

They began by generating a list of questions they would have to answer:

How to construct shelter?
Grow food?
Govern?
Meet basic needs?
Ensure our survival?
Appoint jobs?

After generating a list of open questions, they prioritized each according to its importance, and developed a list of "needs" versus "wants" so they could converge around what was most important. Finding food and water was priority #1.

And while their team of teacher-facilitators had a hunch they might land on food and water as the most important priorities, they didn't force the process. They understood the importance of allowing learners to arrive at this key inquiry on their own. And given most 12-year-olds knew only little about food production, the teachers prepared the relevant activities and experiences to help them explore. Teachers introduced a key anchor text to unpack four major models of food production; invited local farmers, and aquaponics/hydroponics experts to demonstrate what they looked like in action; and organized mini-lessons and proposal-writing workshops for students to create their own.

Through each activity, experience, lesson, or workshop, learners deepened their inquiries. Learner questions developed in complexity, and incorporated the same vocabulary and thought processes of the disciplines they were attempting to emulate. Through a horticulturist lens, students began to inquire about the method of food production that would "create the greatest yield." Through a governance lens, they inquired around which methods of governance would "lead to the greatest societal advancements."

Students acted as inquirers, researchers, and creators all at once because the learning experience demanded it.

In stage 2 of the guided inquiry process, teams of learners put on their effective communicator lens in order to gain approval from the class for their proposed food production and governance models. In order to write their proposals, a plethora of new inquiries surfaced:

How to structure a proposal?
Persuade others?
Address counter-arguments and offer rebuttals?
Speak compellingly?
Incorporate evidence?

Below is a simple diagram to demonstrate the stages of inquiry within a learning experience or unit of study (Image 2.3). "Divergent" lines offer opportunities for open questions with limited parameters, while "convergent lines" represent opportunities for guided or structured inquiry around key activities, experiences, experiments, or readings to develop student questions.

The Open Inquiry Process

On a brisk, sunny morning in Australia, 45 young people stood outside the gates of their campus, holding signs with bold demands:

"Ban single use plastic"
"Stop polluting our oceans"
"Create a carbon tax"
"Protect our marine life"

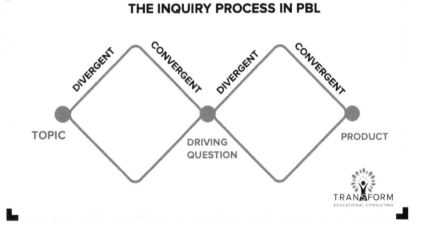

IMAGE 2.3 The Inquiry Process in PBL

Three thousand miles away, on the other side of the world, five young people stood on the Harbourfront of Hong Kong with similar demands. They were hoping to lower Hong Kong's high carbon footprint. They handed each passerby a short poll and questionnaire to identify where they might reduce their l impact on the environment. On a folded piece of cardboard, each participant signed a new pledge to turn that promise into action.

These young citizen groups were self-organized; spanning multiple ages, ethnicities, and demographics; with campaigns they developed entirely on their own. The only adult support they received was in providing a space for them to meet, and a car to drive them to the right location.

It was a youth-led movement that spanned the globe.

Inside Rosie Howes's Grade 1 democratic classroom in Australia, the youth-led movement began with a simple inquiry.

What topics do you want to explore?

It wasn't climate change.

It was Spiderman, dogs, and future worlds. Some even wanted to learn about "poo." Rosie's job as a facilitator was to "find the common themes."

She admits this process is sometimes difficult. "Sometimes these discussions would take an hour, and it would get to the point where you're overwhelmed by so many ideas and looking for themes … it takes some time and energy but the engagement from the students is magical."

The class finally decided on animals. They were especially interested in learning more about the aquatic ones that resided in the ocean nearby.

Rosie organized a trip to the local aquarium, and even had a parent scuba diver visit her classroom to share underwater marine life he encountered during dives. With each experience, students developed new inquiries.

"How do animals breathe underwater?"

"What makes sharks so dangerous?"

"How do whales communicate?"

Rosie encouraged her young learners to discover answers on their own. She set up stations with picture books, learning materials, and hands-on activities to help dive deeper into their inquiries.

Throughout the process, Rosie acted as a careful facilitator and observer, recording student progress toward various learning goals and identifying where there seemed to be the most synergy.

And when it came time for students to take action, they had transformed from passive six- and seven-year-olds into active, informed marine biologists.

The worldwide climate strike in Sydney, Australia, was a coordinated effort to help protect their local marine life by raising awareness in their community.

I can probably predict what you are thinking.

This sounds incredibly powerful, but I've got standards to cover and learning goals to meet. Rosie does as well. And she admits that this can be challenging. "Sometimes it's not always possible [to bring in your curriculum]. Sometimes when you are going with it, it's not going to cover everything … but I'm constantly looking at those objectives and thinking, what are they showing me? What are they showcasing here? What standards can I actually tick off?"

Rosie did more than tick off standards. She built skills and habits in her students that transferred into other units of study, and learning experiences they would undertake on their own: Skills like self-management, prioritization, efficacy, curiosity, collaboration.

Rosie's example shows us the empowerment we provide students by making one simple shift: Leading learning not with mandated content; but through inquiry, integrating curriculum where it best fits.

But leading with inquiry requires more than simply asking students what they want to learn about.

Ask middle or high school students what they want to learn about and you will probably get 25 blank stares and an apathetic shrug. I witnessed one teacher try to get her packed classroom of seventh graders to care more about food waste by spreading the contents of the trash can across the floor. Instead of questions, she got students reminiscing about how hungry they were.

Like co-design, leading with inquiry requires us as facilitators to create an environment that fosters it. Rosie used learning stations and trips to the aquarium to prompt inquiry around aquatic life; Early Years teachers in Pakistan used pictures of nearby communities devastated by floods to prompt inquiry around natural disasters. That same seventh-grade teacher mentioned earlier elicited far more questions when she took students to the nearby beach to do a cleanup.

These guided forms of inquiry help pave the way for more open, student-centered inquiry.

Walk into any student-centered environment and you will probably witness various levels of inquiry happening at the same time. In Rosie's student-centered classroom, she might lay out a more structured inquiry process for some learners using anchor charts and visuals to help students develop questions and project ideas. For students with increased ability in self-management and basic research, she might provide a digital process guide that allows them to move through the extended learning experience at their own pace. And finally, for learners with a strong background and interest in the topic being explored, she might allow them to form teams and formulate *big* questions they hope to explore; and the procedures, milestones, and activities they will undergo to answer it.

Just like co-creation, inquiry runs on a student-centric continuum. Using it effectively requires a delicate balance of of both teacher and self-guidance, depending on the needs of the experience and learners.

Transforming a Traditional Unit to Be Inquiry-Based

Enter Michelle Willis's tenth-grade English classroom.

Michelle is a great teacher. She builds strong relationships with learners and always generates lively discussions when exploring themes in Literature.

And like many other American literature classrooms, *The Great Gatsby* was atop the reading list. But here was the rub: Michelle's students don't live in the mansions of Long Island, New York; they live in small apartment buildings in Southeast San Diego. How were students of color supposed to relate to, or care about the lives of rich white families born into "old money" in Long Island, New York?

Teaching *The Great Gatsby* was always an uphill battle for Michelle.

Michelle tried her best. Given her ability to connect with learners of all backgrounds, she asked students to critically analyze representations of the American Dream found in the novel and compare and contrast them to the realities of today. Students wrote book reports and essays sharing their thoughts, using evidence from the text to support their reasoning.

Yet while the assignment involved critical analysis and honored student voice, it engaged, like so many literature classes, a very small cross- section of students. Most students were tuned out from chapter 1. She needed a better hook. And similar to the edu-transformers introduced earlier in the chapter, she found it in an open inquiry.

What if instead of writing book reports, students acted as anthropologists to capture their own communities' version of the American Dream? What if they shared these stories in a community forum accessible to all?

The seedling for a six-week inquiry-based experience was born.

Instead of starting the unit with *The Great Gatsby*, she started with a question.

As writers, how can uncovering and sharing stories from our community help us re-imagine the American Dream?

Her students immediately sprung to action. They didn't go to the rich neighborhoods on the coast to interview the wealthy;

but to their own extended families' rundown apartment buildings to uncover stories they had never heard before. They learned about grandparents who migrated to the United States from Mexico with nothing but the clothes on their back, and community organizers who took ou small loans to run after-school programs for disadvantaged youth.

They also uncovered stories whose "American Dream" turned out to be an "American Nightmare": Older siblings who became responsible for parenting their entire family; those who never earned a high school diploma because they spent most of their childhood working full-time to put food on their family's table.

Students contrasted these stories with the ones they found in the novel. It became clear that they needed a new narrative for the "American Dream" in 2023. Michelle asked students to consider how they might share the stories they uncovered.

Some suggested a class book. But that idea had limited reach.

Some suggested making videos. But that idea required lots of equipment.

Some suggested making a mural. But that idea failed to capture the depth of the stories.

Then one shy, soft-spoken girl volunteered her idea.

"Well, I have my own podcast. Perhaps we can make an 'American Dream' podcast, with each episode featuring a different community story."

The class erupted in unanimous approval. Suddenly it wasn't a static assignment that would engage the top 10 percent of learners. To make a polished, professional podcast, it was going to require the talents of an entire classroom full of aspiring podcast producers.

Each episode would feature the perfect blend of these talents in small teams. One student would be responsible for cover art, one for music/sound effects, one for the interview, and one for mixing and editing it all together.

New inquiries emerged.

What is the perfect podcast episode length? What makes for a good interview question? How do you help guests prepare? What is the best mixing and editing software? What effect does the title of a podcast have on the number of downloads? How do you market podcasts?

Through the inquiry process, Michelle was able to shift from a teacher to a gentle guide.

She developed helpful Digital Guides to support students in generating questions, conducting research, synthesizing information, and putting together episodes. She hosted literature circle discussions with small groups of students to help them identify motifs and consider how they might be used in their own work. She developed project folders to keep track of each team's work and ensure they made progress. She hosted lunch meetings for podcast committees to agree upon titles, distribution channels, cover art, and descriptions.

Michelle became a stagehand, while her students became the main actors.

They took full ownership.

They stayed in during lunch and after school to edit episodes. Stayed up late at night to generate original beats. Built soundproof soundscapes in different wings of the school to record interviews.

They even worked together as a class to film the podcast video trailer and post it to YouTube: Turning ownership over to students, Michelle is seen at her desk, with a student taking on the teacher role from the front of the room. In a tired, old voice, he asks the class to turn to page 45 of their novels, and right on cue the class erupts into chaos. A new student steps into the "teacher role" and breaks into a fully choreographed dance and rap to introduce their new project. The class joins along.

Leading learning with inquiry is *magic*.

But it isn't without its shortcomings. It's hard to get unanimity on a cohesive idea when opening up possibilities to the class, and it would be disingenuous to say that 100 percent of students bought into the podcast idea. Some were brilliant writers, and they also wanted a space for their unique talents to shine.

Michelle worked with these students to find a space for their voices. Many found it in writing their own original blog posts to share their personal stories of the American Dream. One girl penned her story about spending her whole life struggling with body image. She re-imagined the American Dream by asking America to expand its definition of beauty to include all sizes.

Michelle is an incredible teacher, but I bet you are just as imaginative.

Leading with inquiry doesn't require you to re-create units from scratch. I'm asking you to make one small creative shift that will turn your students from passive learners to active, engaged citizens.

And here's the simple formula. Are you ready?

Draw three circles. Label one "curriculum." Label one "community needs." Label one "student and teacher interest."

Place the unit you would like to shift into becoming more learner-centered in the curriculum circle.

Place a community need related to that unit concept, topic, title, or idea into the "community need" circle.

Finally, place the relevant student/teacher interests into the third circle.

Next, write an essential/driving inquiry question that merges the three.

In need of more examples? I've got tons of them in the next section.

Developing Driving/Essential Questions

Michelle's "re-defining" the "American Dream" experience was driven by one *big* question. In the project-based learning world, these are called Driving Questions. In the IB world, these are called Essential Questions or Statements of Inquiry. While I have had experience developing both, I must admit my strong bias toward creating questions rather than statements. Statements don't inspire students to incorporate their own voices/interests and ideas. They are designed to guide students in confirming the statement. It's the old-fashioned game we have always played in school called "Try to guess what the teacher wants you to understand." And while it's presented in a more interesting, conceptual form, it's still teacher-centric.

Questions invite input. They ask learners to derive their own conclusions and develop their own unique ways of answering them.

But not all questions are created equally. Closed questions still play the game of "Guess what's in the teacher's head."

The best questions are open and inviting.

After working for 15 years with teachers to develop essential questions, I have narrowed them down to five traits that inspire W-O-N-D-E-R.

Worthwhile: Essential questions should be worthwhile answering. They should ask students to address a problem/challenge that puts them in the shoes of real experts in the field. They should require acting as real historians, mathematicians, anthropologists, authors, scientists, or engineers to answer them.

Open-Ended: Great questions allow for multiple answers that are equally correct. These answers can't be Googled, Binged, or Chat GPT'd. They are often action-oriented. Asking students to solve problems in new, novel ways. Think, "How can we … ?"

'Need to Know' for Acquisition of Content/Skills: While great essential/driving questions should be accessible to the learner, they should also require deep investigation to answer. In this way, content found in a textbook, curriculum guide, the internet, or through an expert becomes more meaningful and integrated in a way that helps the learner develop answers for themselves.

Dictate Parameters: While great questions are open-ended, in the case of inquiry- or project-based experiences, they also provide parameters to ensure deeper, meaningful learning. They are not the source of endless hours of philosophical debate and ramblings; but rather action-oriented around specific, tangible problems or ideas. For example, rather than say, "How do we solve global warming?" they instead read, "How might we lower our carbon footprint at home and school?"

Easy to Understand: Great questions are accessible to the learners we teach. While we might ask Year 7 or 8 students, "How do we use principles of entrepreneurship to meet a community need?" For second grade students, we might ask, "How can green spaces lead to happy faces?"

Relevant: Great driving/essential questions are relevant to students' lives and the communities in which they live. It would be far more relevant to ask students with limited recreation space "how to increase play space" than it would be to ask a question around designing a new amusement park.

Here are some sample driving questions:

- How do we use the principles of entrepreneurship to meet a community need?
- What impact do humans have on our local watershed, and how can we better protect them?
- How can we use public spaces to show how life is different for people on the other side of the border?
- How can sharing stories of immigration help reverse stereotypes we see?
- How can we demystify coronavirus vaccines in order to help people make informed decisions about their health?
- How can "green spaces" lead to happier faces?
- What makes a hero, and how can we best celebrate them within our communities?
- How do we re-create the values of society from the artifacts they carried with them?
- How do we use data to make a positive impact on a local waterway?
- How can we plant positive seeds of culture that will grow and flourish for years to come?
- How can we create an affordable play area that is safe and accessible to all students?
- How do circuits improve our lives?
- How can humans create sustainable and efficient modern ecosystems?

The Power of Provocations

Many educators make the mistake of launching the inquiry process with a single question. And while some questions have the power to inspire and captivate students, most of them won't be hooked by a question. They will be hooked by an experience.

In the world of Reggio Emilia and Montessori education, these are called "provocations."

Provocations are intended to provoke curiosity, wonder, and further questions.

An engineering provocation might include laying out a series of arts and crafts materials and asking students to build a small bridge across two tables. This provocation might lead to a deeper inquiry around:

"How as engineers can we improve the design and safety of play structures at our school?"

A biology provocation might include a short "bio-blitz" in a natural area behind school for students to capture plant and animal life. This provocation could lead to a deeper inquiry around:

"How can we protect and preserve the biodiversity around our school?"

A narrative writing provocation might include creating baggies of items and asking students to write stories around them. This provocation might lead to a deeper inquiry around:

"How, as creative storytellers, can we share stories of heroes in our community?"

These examples are all taken from student-centered classrooms that span multiple ages and subjects.

Do they guide students to a predetermined outcome? Yes.

Is it completely student-led? No.

But unless you teach in an after school program or elective with minimal curricular or assessment requirements, there is going to be some teacher- guided inquiry. Especially at the onset.

And if you recall from the initial allegory that started this chapter, learners are going to benefit from a leash before being set free to roam wild. That is what the essential inquiry or driving question provides. It's an anchor that helps provide grounding for the deeper learning students will engage in.

With an essential question in place, students will naturally develop questions of their own. In the question around entrepreneurship, students explored local businesses they admired and inquired around how did they turn profits? Benefit the community? Develop their products? Advertise? Grow/scale operations? Answering these questions helped them better understand how to build their own businesses. In the big question around living history museums, students explored how museums were curated. Inquired about the components of effective exhibits. Asked how historians pieced together history to re-create important events, lessons, and people? At the same time, they used answers to these questions to curate their own exhibits.

If you develop an essential question that hooks learners, you won't have to spend as much time coercing students into "finding something they love." It will happen naturally. That girl who shows up each day with a new outfit, and spends her free time snapping selfies with friends in the hall can resurrect Civil War–era fashion trends; while the aspiring young disc jockey can re-imagine authentic 19th century backing tracks for Civil War battle scenes.

As facilitator, your role is to uncover those inquiries, and let curiosity guide the process. Lessons will no longer be guided by the next chapter of the textbook, but by each successive inquiry students choose to explore. With your North Star in place (the essential/driving question), you can rest assured that students won't drift too far off course.

Inquiry Journals

The inquiry process can be incredibly hard to manage; especially if students are investigating the central inquiry question according to their own unique lens, insights, and ideas. How do you support students in owning and documenting their own journey?

This is a question Chris Gadbury, a student-centered Primary Years Program Arts teacher became obsessed with when considering how to develop individualized inquiry in his classroom. His solution was a beautifully constructed inquiry journal that takes students through the entire process of inquiry, from initial question to relevant activities, experiments, research, subquestions, idea frames, milestones, and reflection to develop it. And while the framework for the journal might be the same, students have total autonomy in how they populate it.

To develop yours, I would begin by populating the major milestones students will reach within the inquiry-based experience. These might include, "proposal submission," "product sketches," "presentation outline," "storyboard." This will help frame the relevant activities, types of inquiry, thinking routines, and tools to help students move to each successive milestone. (More on developing milestones in Chapter 4.) Next, populate the space between milestones with space for student reflection, new questions and insights.

These journals will not only help guide learners through the inquiry process, but also help you in maintaining your sanity! With 25-plus learners all responding to the inquiry with their own unique ideas, products, insights, solutions, and lens, you can have a central place to house them. And while the learning process wil surely be messy, the journals will help tell a cohesive story of growth and development.

There's more around inquiry journals and several other simple tools to help learners manage the inquiry process in Chapter 7, "Student Reflection."

Finally, let's return to the metaphor of the unleashed dogs that launched this chapter. I want you to imagine a classroom full of learners with their leashes removed, guided by the invisible hand of inquiry and wonder. Some engage in in-depth research on Chromebooks in the corner; others build cardboard prototypes of novel ideas and solutions at tables to the side; some write ideas and questions in response to a prompt at standing whiteboards at the front.

Does your classroom look similar? How might you take the learning from this chapter to begin lengthening your leash?

In the next chapter we will explore what happens when we remove the leash entirely—and move from teacher guided inquiry to unbridled student-led inquiry.

Take the Inquiry Scorecard

LEARNING PROCESS

	Led by Content <--> Led by Inquiry				NOW	NEXT
	1	2	3	4		
	Seedling (Sower)	Budding (Builder)	Blossoming (Beacon)	Flourishing (Facilitator)		
Learning Process	Academic Content is the main driver of learning, with disconnected activities and lessons. Projects tagged on at the end.	Learning Experiences are built around academic content. And while content aligns, inquiry does not guide the experience, only fulfillment of tasks to meet academic criteria.	Learning Experiences have a central inquiry and there are some processes, templates, and activities to drive student inquiry. But inquiry is not ongoing and continuous.	Though there are milestones, inquiry drives the progression to each milestone. There are continual processes, templates, and activities to support and develop student inquiry through literature, expanded research, connection to experts, and field experiences. Teacher acts as a facilitator in the process, connecting student interest and passion to larger, deeper inquiries.		

Reflective Questions

1. How might you capture and develop student questions, wonderings, and inquiries?
2. What's a current lesson or unit you teach? How might you transform it to becoming more inquiry-based?
3. Is inquiry structured, guided, or open in your classroom? What steps would you have to take to move to more open inquiry?
4. What kind of questions do you pose? Are they "closed" or "open"? What impact might modeling an inquiry approach have on your learners?

See Image 2.4 for inquiry strategies and concepts introduced in the chapter.

CONTENT BASED
APPROACH

GUIDED BY CONTENT

CONTENT LEA

TEACHERS QUESTIONS

LEARNING IS SEQUENTIAL

SHALLOW INVESTIGATION

MULTIPL

CLOSED/ FIXED QUESTIONS

FIXED ANSWERS

HIDDE THINKI

LEARNING IS DISCONNECTED

@kwagssd3

© 2020 Kyle Wagner and Rob Riordan

TRANSFORM
EDUCATIONAL CONSULTING

IMAGE 2.4 Shift 2/3 Inquiry-Based Approach Infographic

INQUIRY BASED
APPROACH

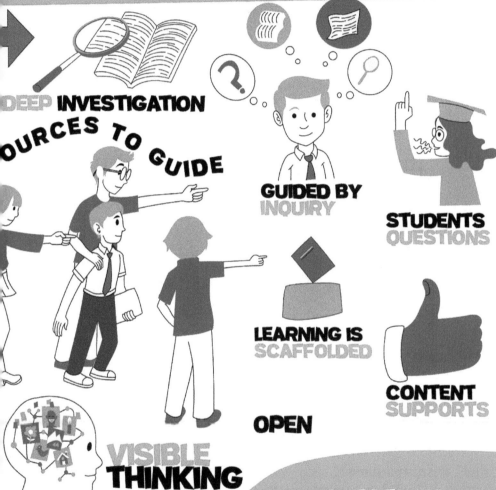

DEEP INVESTIGATION

OURCES TO GUIDE

GUIDED BY INQUIRY

STUDENTS QUESTIONS

LEARNING IS SCAFFOLDED

CONTENT SUPPORTS

OPEN

VISIBLE THINKING

QUESTIONS

LEARNING IS EXPLORATORY

A   B   C

MULTIPLE ANSWERS

3

Shift #3: From Teacher-Led Inquiry to Student-Led Inquiry

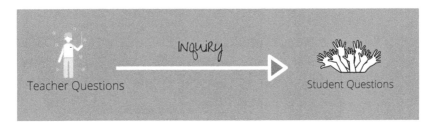

IMAGE 3.1 Shift 3 Building Student Inquiry

> What effect does the material of a swimsuit have on the speed of a swimmer
>
> —Year 7 student- generated inquiry question

"Any questions?"

I used to hate this question. My high school physics teacher would always ask it after drawing up some complicated equations on the board. I'm sure I wasn't the only one who had questions, but I definitely wasn't going to raise my hand and ask them in that setting.

After seeing that there were no questions, our teacher would give himself a satisfied grin and tell us that we had the next 30 minutes to finish the corresponding exercises in our textbook. I remember clumsily fumbling through the exercises. Sometimes

DOI: 10.4324/9781003398226-5

I managed to plug in the right variables or magically stumble upon the right answer; but most of the time I had no idea what I was doing. I have a hunch that the rest of the class didn't either.

I also remember receiving a B+ in that class. How I earned such a high mark is more a reflection of the mindless tasks I was asked to fulfill rather than the learning that occurred. I couldn't tell you about the relationship of forces, motion, acceleration, frequency, or angular motion; all I could do was plug variables into equations and derive an unknown quantity that was correct some of the time.

"Any questions" is more a question that seeks affirmation than it does novel, student-generated inquiry.

But my high school physics teacher wasn't the only one who uttered that phrase from the front of the classroom. As a new teacher, I used the phrase on a daily basis. And like him, I was only seeking questions around things I already knew.

Our kids come to school with millions of questions. And most of the time, they aren't related to our content.

They have questions about their future careers.

How to get more people at school to like them.

How to gain the confidence and skills to make the sports team or gain a spot in an exclusive after-school club.

Questions around how to fix a bike, make money, or plan a summer vacation.

But we aren't going to discover any of these questions with a didactic mode of delivery.

Last chapter we discussed how to lead learning experiences primarily through teacher-guided inquiry. In this chapter, we will explore how to help students discover and explore their own inquiries; how to let curiosity and imagination lead them to new, more developed questions; and how to build a learning environment that invites wonder and curiosity.

John Chau had just finished mounting his iPad atop a tall tripod next to the net of an indoor tennis court. He pressed the large black circle at the bottom of the screen. The flashing red light indicated that the recording had begun. The sun bathed the tennis court in a warm glow. John's tennis partner stood motionless. With a steady hand, John adjusted the settings on his mechanical friend, fine-tuning the speed and trajectory. Anticipation filled the air as he prepared to engage in a solitary dance with his relentless mechanical partner. John's scientific experiment would finally begin.

Welcome to a self-guided learning experience led entirely by student inquiry. The question John was exploring:

"Does string tension impact my tennis performance?" His playing partner was a tennis ball machine.

This was experiment #1 with loosely wound strings. John would conduct three more experiments, each with a slightly tighter stringed racket. One iPad would record his motion, ball trajectory, and location of each shot; while another connected to an app that was able to measure velocity, height, and shot accuracy. At home, John would spend time analyzing each video and jot down the recorded information into a spreadsheet. John would need this information to summarize and graph his results in science class the next day.

But it wasn't only John leading his own investigation. Other Year 7 learners were investigating inquiries of their own. A studious, brown-haired, brown-eyed girl wanted to investigate the effect of regular travel on performance in her geography class. She had a hunch that international students, given their extensive travel experience, would tend to perform better. She was right. They scored twice as high on the geography test she administered than their non-traveling peers.

Another gregarious aqua enthusiast wanted to test the effects of swimsuit fabric on her swimming speed. Her inquiry: "How does the material of a swimsuit affect the speed of a swimmer?" After researching the science behind swimsuit design, she predicted that FastSkin swimsuits would result in significantly faster speeds than traditional bathing suits. After conducting her experiment, she concluded that they made only a minor difference.

In the process of taking on their own inquiries, students learned about dependent and independent variables; control versus experimental groups; research bias; qualitative versus quantitative data collection; the graphing of data; and other mandated skills as part of the Year 7 science curriculum. But more importantly, they learned how to develop their own open-ended inquiries and follow them to novel conclusions.

This is the power of leading learning with student versus teacher questions. And with the right prompting, we can elicit those questions, regardless of the subject.

Here's where to start:

Before introducing a new concept, topic, or idea to students, discover what students may already know and what questions they have. Write the topic on the board and create three quadrants stemming off the topic entitled Think, Puzzle, Explore. After distributing colored sticky notes, ask students to jot down what they think they know, what puzzles they have, and how they might explore those puzzles. Next, have them place the stickies in the respective quadrants on the board. For example, if the topic is Space Exploration, perhaps they "think they know" that Mercury is the closest planet to the sun, are "puzzled" why Mars can't support life forms and want to "explore" that puzzle by watching short, animated videos on planetary composition. After gathering these puzzles, you, as a facilitator, can begin to categorize them. What are students most interested in exploring? What themes emerge in their wonderings?

This thinking routine is not my own. It is one of several thinking routines put out by Project Zero at Harvard Graduate School of Education to elicit student inquiry and make their thinking visible. Other routines include See, Think, Wonder, Circle of Viewpoints, and Claim, Support, Question. Integrating these thinking routines in your classroom will shift learning from one of surface-level questions and answers to one of deep inquiry and exploration.

There are other routines that allow us to remove ourselves entirely from the equation. One of my favorite thinking routines to elicit this student-centered inquiry is entitled "chalk talk." This routine asks students to consider their own ideas, questions, or connections by silently responding in writing to specific prompts, as well as to the ideas of others. As facilitators, we have only to prepare the classroom by placing these questions/ prompts onto large pieces of butcher/chart paper around the room. Equipped with a poster marker and their ability to think critically, students move to each prompt and respond with their own thoughts, insights, or inquiries. As the chart paper begins to fill, more sub-ideas and questions emerge to respond to. Before long, the entire paper is filled with student thinking.

I witnessed a beautiful implementation of this activity in a high school history class around the American Dream. Students circulated around the room and responded to relevant prompts including:

1. Is the American Dream still alive?
2. What does the American Dream mean to you?
3. Who has access to the American Dream?

In response to question #1, one student wrote, "for some people." In response to that statement, someone wrote, "who?" Another student generated a sub-question: "How has the American Dream changed?"

In response to prompt #2, one student wrote "happiness." Another student wrote, "What is happiness?" In response, another student wrote, "financial freedom." Another student asked, "What makes someone financially free?"

After time had elapsed for the activity, the teacher facilitated a deeper discussion around each prompt through the responses students had given. There was a noticeable shift in the level of student engagement in the inquiry process. Prior to the activity, there was dead air in the room; now it was filled with the buzz of student discussion and critical reasoning.

The QFT Method: Co-creating *Big* Questions with Learners

We often ask students to be "thoughtful inquirers" without teaching them how to develop thoughtful questions. Think back to your own experience with question formation. Did you come up with the right question for your master's thesis or doctoral study in a day? In my master's work on democratic classrooms, it took six months! It required clarity around what I was hoping to find and regular discussion with my adviser on what questions to ask to uncover it. Unfortunately, most of us don't have that kind of time for exploration with our own students. But what if we could provide students with a repeatable framework to support their own question formation in a few steps, leading to inquiries that supported deep, sustained investigation over an extended period of time.?

We spoke a lot about how to introduce processes that develop inquiries within our classrooms; now it's time to explore student-centered inquiry across an entire school.

This is the ethos of Innovations Academy, a K–8 charter school in San Diego, California. While a Year 5 classroom investigates the effect of music on overall health and well-being, a kindergarten classroom explores how our daily choices are affecting the local bee population. While a Year 4 classroom investigates how to use light and sound to communicate emotion, a Year 2 classroom explores the impact our families have on personal identity. At the same time a Year 6 classroom investigates the math behind the most-beloved community businesses, a Year 1 classroom investigates how to increase resilience by studying Emperor penguins.

Most of the questions that launch these expeditions were co-crafted with learner input:

> *How can we improve the lives of our local butterflies?*
> *How can storytelling inspire people to take better care of their environment?*
> *How does our family history impact who we are today?*
> *How can we use light and sound to communicate emotion through art?*
> *How can understanding math help us develop viable community business plans?*
> *What can we learn about resilience from studying Emperor penguins?*

And while many grade levels take an organic approach in question formation, some take a more systematic, structured approach called Question Formulation Technique (QFT) to ensure students land on the "right question" to explore. Developed by the Right Question Institute, the QFT method "distills sophisticated forms of divergent, convergent, and metacognitive thinking into a simple, accessible and reproducible technique." Through developing the central question, students learn to "think critically, feel greater power and self-efficacy, and become more confident and ready to participate in civic life."

Here's how to use the approach in developing questions with your learners.

Step #1: Begin with a provocation, or what the Right Institute calls a QFocus. This could be an image, video, phrase, statement, mural, math problem, equation, object, or other provocation that gets questions flowing. In most cases, this provocation is related to a topic, unit, or piece of content you have to teach. For example, if planning to study living and non-living things, the QFocus could be an aquarium or a self-contained ecosystem.

Step #2: Ask students to generate as many questions as they can related to the QFocus. Similar to a quick write, there's no stopping to edit or judge question quality; the focus is on quantity. After time has elapsed, students number their questions in preparation for Step Two.

Step #3: Ask students to categorize questions as either "open" or "closed." While open questions allow for multiple answers and require explanation, closed questions can be answered with a simple "yes," "no," or one word. After students finish marking each question, discuss the advantages and disadvantages of each question type. You might explain that closed questions are best for foundational knowledge gathering, while open questions allow for new knowledge to be built. Have them practice changing questions from closed to open and open to closed to examine the effect it might have on their inquiry.

Step #4: The next step is for question prioritization. Have learners choose three questions that they think will be most useful for deeper research, for the design of an experiment, or for addressing a problem. Generally, these questions can include many of their closed questions. For example, "What impacts do humans have on our natural environment?" includes closed questions like, "What organisms make up our natural environment?"

Usually, this is where the QFT process ends; I would suggest, however, adding one more step:

Step #5: Consolidating learner questions into a collective inquiry question for the whole class to explore. Adding this step will help foster interdependence in addressing a shared challenge, provocation, or cause. Collect each learner's three questions and rewrite them on the board. Next, write the following sentence stem:

How (might we) (can) _____ help _____ ?
    (What they will investigate)   (hoped learning outcome)

Point out patterns or themes you notice in the questions they wrote. Invite them to share the similarities they notice in the questions. Finally, work with them to create one central question that encapsulates these themes and hoped learning outcome (s).

Using the QFT process or other processes for generating student inquiry transforms our students from passive recipients into active, engaged inquirers. But it doesn't just transform our students. It also transforms us. Facilitating this process transforms us from deliverers of content to provocateurs of questions. As provocateurs, we are able to elicit inquiry and channel it in a pathway that hits key learning objectives while also honoring our learners' unique interests.

What's Next? From Inquiry to Investigation: How to Support Learners in Investigating Their Questions

We have spoken a lot about helping learners frame questions. But what's next? How do we support students in answering them? What does it look like when 25 students pursue 25 unique questions for an extended period of time?!

We can't possibly support them all. After all, there's only one of us.

This is the mindset of a teacher-centered practitioner: One who views themselves as the channel for all knowledge and learning. But what if we empowered our learners to take charge of their own learning process? After writing big questions, what if they self-identified gaps in knowledge, sought the necessary resources to fill them, and developed projects to put the learning into action?

This is what learner-centered practitioner, and cohort leader Jonathan Lee Campbell has empowered his students to do through the design thinking process. Design thinking provides a powerful, repeatable framework for self-guided exploration.

The design thinking process helps one student explore how to make fashion more affordable for the local community. Their How Might We (HMW) question: "How might we fashionably upcycle clothes to make fashion more affordable?"

It's helping another explore how to help more abandoned pets find homes. Their HMW question, "How might we design a doghouse that will help others adopt dogs?"

It's helping another explore the effects of lights on children's sleep. Their HMW question, "How might we create lighting patterns that help children sleep better?"

The Design Thinking Process helps learners journey through five powerful steps of exploration: Empathize, Define, Ideate, Prototype, and Test. In the "empathy" stage, learners explore a cause or challenge personally meaningful to them. Through interviews, observations, and guided research, they gather insights that help them understand the users most affected. In the "define," stage, they synthesize their findings and develop a "how might we" question to frame their insights into a simple provocation for how to positively impact those users. Next, they "ideate" several ideas or projects that might benefit them. During the "prototype" phase, with the support of expert mentors, they build out solutions. These can be hand-made, digital, written, or other products. Finally, in the "test" phase, they test out their prototypes and gain feedback from the user they designed for.

Students are using the Design Thinking Process to build community gardens; clean water filters; upcycle clothing; stage photography exhibitions; and more.

As a learner-centered practitioner, JC (Jonathan Campbell) admits that this kind of self-guided learning takes time.

"Students need to go through the process several times before they are able to do it on their own."

To familiarize students with the process, JC first takes students through guided challenges. These range from creating community maps to growing vegetables on the rooftop. Throughout the challenge, John uses guided activities and templates to support learners in progressing to each successive step. This Gradual Increase of Independence, adapted from Pearson and Gallagher's Gradual Release of Responsibility scale, helps equip learners to soon be, as JC puts it, "at the center of their learning."

Remember the leash metaphor at the beginning of the chapter? Not all learners are Candys, who are ready to roam free the minute you let them off the leash. Some are Daisys. The leashes are structures and processes like these that help them find their way back home when they are finally let off.

By moving from guided to open inquiry through design thinking, JC is empowering all of his learners to roam free.

Letting Learners Completely off the Leash

You have your own learners and unique context. You also have unique constraints. Not all schools and systems allow for, or even believe in, unrestrained open inquiry.

But as learner-centered practitioners, I am hoping this is our goal.

When the confines of a classroom are removed, and our learners move on to pursuing their own inquiries and goals, will they be ready? Will they know how to pursue their own questions and seek out their own resources?

The greatest tragedy of a teacher-centered classroom is extinguishing the natural wonderment and curiosity of its learners. By creating an environment that not only invites wonderment and curiosity, but also provides a sandbox for developing it, we will have paved the way for lifelong, self-directed learning.

Shift #3: Inquiry: From Teacher Questions to Student Questions

Teacher Inquiry < -- >Student Questions

	1	2	3	4	Now	Next
	Seedling (Sower)	Budding (Builder)	Blossoming (Beacon)	Flourishing (Facilitator)		
Inquiry	Questions are "closed" in learning experiences and start and end with teacher questions.	Facilitator provides more open-ended questions and opportunities for inquiry, but little to no support in the process of discovering answers.	Innovative Facilitator helps facilitate student inquiry and lets the questions drive the process, but does little to develop student questions with protocols, structures, processes and experiences.	Students drive their own learning experiences through deep inquiry, with the teacher establishing routines, protocols, forums, and processes to extend and support it.		

Reflective Questions

1. What inquiry processes from this chapter might support you within your own classroom?
2. How might you develop student questions? How might you make student questions and inquiries more visible?
3. How will understanding what students are curious about help you co-design learning experiences with them?

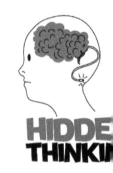

IMAGE 3.2 Shift 2/3 Inquiry-Based Approach Infographic

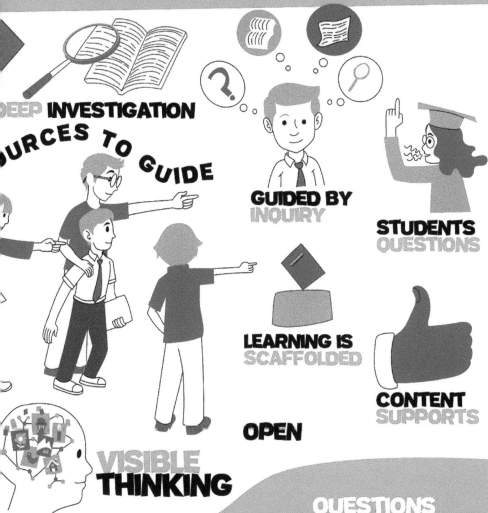

INQUIRY BASED
APPROACH

DEEP INVESTIGATION

SOURCES TO GUIDE

GUIDED BY INQUIRY

STUDENTS QUESTIONS

LEARNING IS SCAFFOLDED

CONTENT SUPPORTS

OPEN

VISIBLE THINKING

LEARNING IS EXPLORATORY

QUESTIONS

A   B   C

MULTIPLE ANSWERS

Bibliography

"Claim, Support, Question." *Project Zero*, pz.harvard.edu/resources/claim-support-question. Accessed 14 Oct. 2023.

4

Shift #4: From Isolated Curriculum and Skills by Discipline to Relevant, Transdisciplinary Skills

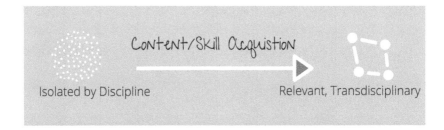

IMAGE 4.1 Shift 4 Interdisciplinary Content and Skill Acquisition

> We need to stop looking at subjects as bodies of knowledge to be transmitted and absorbed, and start seeing them as powerful lenses for understanding the world.
> —Rob Riordan, High Tech High Co-founder and President Emeritus

Four adults huddle around a large writable table with a stack of Post-Its in their hand.

One scribbles down an idea while another excitedly announces, "Growable gardens for the school."

They slam their Post-It note down on the table.

DOI: 10.4324/9781003398226-6

The one who was scribbling their idea draws a line through one word, adds another to the end and then shouts, *"Yes, and students can explore other renewable systems like waste, food, and energy."*

Another adult in blue khaki shorts and a short sleeved Hawaiian T-shirt exclaims, "Viable systems for the new boarding school."

All four sets of eyeballs widen. The energy is palpable. They have discovered an idea worth exploring.

This is not a brainstorming session at IDEO, Google, or Apple headquarters. It's a brainstorm around potential learning experiences conducted in the flexible meeting space of an innovative International School.

Welcome to the Year 7/8 Verso International School Interdisciplinary Team planning session.

The adults huddled around the table have willingly given up their "teacher" title in exchange for one more relevant to what they are trying to achieve: Learning Designers. As learning designers, they take the responsibility to connect their content to learning experiences that move beyond the traditional confines of their subjects. As a result they have organized learning not in short, disconnected 45-minute chunks of time for math, science, art, humanities, languages, and PE, but instead, around larger blocks of time for these experiences to take flight, called Learning Labs.

Over the course of this particular Learning Lab, students will be tasked with developing the plan and proposal for the new boarding school they will inhabit. Do you recall the previous chapters on leading learning via inquiry rather than content? This interdisciplinary experience will also be guided by a big question:

"How can understanding closed loop systems help us develop viable communities of the future?"

Verso has unlocked the three magic ingredients for authentic, interdisciplinary experiences:

A deep, meaningful question.
An authentic, student-centered outcome.
A relevant, interdisciplinary body of content and skills.

In eight weeks' time, students will present their plans for a viable, closed-loop boarding school to the architects and engineers tasked to build it.

Learning designers are handling their curriculum in the same way my dear mentor Rob Riordan of High Tech High asked me to treat my humanities curriculum 15 years ago; "Not as a body of knowledge, but as a lens to see the world."

I wonder what might happen if we viewed our curriculum through the same lens? What subject do you teach? How might it fit within this experience?

Let's start with the math lens. For this Learning Lab, Ashley Durdle, the Maths Learning Designer, highlighted parts of her curriculum that included mathematical modeling. Students would need to understand the reasoning behind mathematical models in order to build viability models for their own. As they explored waste, energy, sewage, water, and other systems, they would use mathematical modeling to ensure they remained in a closed loop.

Through the Science Lens, Shanna Comeford, the Humanities/Science Learning Designer, highlighted parts of her curriculum that included energy transfers, systems, and management. Students would need to explore these concepts in order to develop infographics for how their systems would function. Students built these infographics in small teams, according to the systems they were most interested in exploring. They also conducted small- scale experiments to better understand energy transfers and regeneration.

Through a language lens, Maria Pannakan, the Language and Learning Support Designer, highlighted parts of her curriculum that included informational writing and argumentative reasoning. Students would need these pieces in order to develop their proposals and defend their models for sustainable, closed-loop systems at the new boarding school.

Finally, through the art and maker lens. Amy Premo, the Arts Learning Designer, in tandem with the Makerspace Learning Design lead, highlighted parts of their curriculum that included perspective/CAD drawing, prototyping, and the engineering design cycle. Students would need these skills to visualize and build three-dimensional representations of their models.

And it wasn't just the LDs (Learning Designers) who would do the teaching in this experience. Students already adept in these skills would act as co-teachers to support their peers in acquiring relevant knowledge, and filling learning gaps.

For eight weeks, students at Verso would be given ongoing opportunities to connect learning and acquire cross-cutting skills in a meaningful way. And at the end of this interdisciplinary journey, it wouldn't be their teacher they were presenting their viable models to, but the actual architects and engineers tasked to build it.

Verso is one of several courageous schools taking an active approach to helping students acquire "skills of the future."

According to a recent report by the World Economic Forum, analytical thinking and innovation, active learning and learning strategies, and complex problem-solving make the top three. Other skills include critical thinking, creativity and initiative, technology design, and programming, among others. Learners at Verso International will require many of these skills when designing their future boarding school.

Their learning will blur the traditional boundaries of disciplines, skill sets, and habits of mind. It reflects the same interdisciplinary, learner-centered environment that they will experience when they leave formal schooling, amid organizations and careers that require a diverse range of skills. And given that active learning is listed as the #2 skill of the future, I imagine their schooling won't end when they leave college.

"How might you use this example to make learning more interdisciplinary in your context? "

Low Stakes Starting Points for Interdisciplinary Learning Experiences

Not all of us have complete autonomy over the learning experiences we design. Some of us have rigid curriculums, fixed schedules, and a pre-established system on how we report. But we can all start somewhere.

We might begin by exploring the connections between cross-cutting concepts.

If you teach at an IB (International Baccalaureate) School with the Primary Years (PYP), Middles Years (MYP), or Diploma Programme (DP) Curriculum, these broader concepts have already been written for us. Cross-cutting concepts like Communities, Connections, Global Interactions, Relationships, and Systems all allow for exploration across multiple subjects' lenses. If you use "Next Generation Science Standards" (NGSS), you have also been given cross-cutting concepts that include "stability and change," "systems and models," and "patterns." If you teach at a public school using Common Core Curriculum, you might begin with cross-cutting skills around "communication," "collaboration," and "critical thinking."

At Colegio Decroly Americano, an international school in Guatemala, secondary learners explored Global Interactions through a geography, economics, policy, and language lens. Using the Russia Invasion of Ukraine as a context, learners analyzed the global interactions disrupted as a result, the economic consequences of strategic alliances, and the resulting policy changes needed to create a resolution.

Through an extended interdisciplinary experience, learners acted as ambassadors to bring their learning together in a United Nations Mock Simulation. But it wasn't just the students who worked together. Their student-centered facilitators (designers) worked together to schedule in time during subject-specific classes to acquire the necessary background knowledge, while developing speeches, position papers, and presentations to be used at the forum.

Did you catch that? Teachers used their *scheduled* subject time to deliver interdisciplinary learning experiences: Zero disruption to the master schedule; zero disruption to the mandated curriculum. The only disruption was in how they organized the learning experiences.

What opportunities exist for this kind of connection in your context? For a student-centered practitioner, it could be simply around a few lessons.

Are you conducting a scientific investigation on the local waterway? How do you plan to have students share their findings?

Connect with the language teacher across the hall to deliver a few lessons around informative writing.

Exploring forces and motions in physics? How will students demonstrate their understanding of each type of reaction? Connect with the design teacher in the underutilized MakerSpace downstairs around how to design simple machines.

Here in Hong Kong, teachers have made some of the most incredible interdisciplinary connections simply by stepping outside their classroom doors. Over a short lunch conversation at an international primary school, a Year 4 science teacher connected with the technology teacher around building sustainable growing spaces. The technology teacher had recently introduced the building of virtual worlds in "co-spaces" (https://cospaces. io/edu/) while the Year 4 teacher had just introduced a study around local organisms. In a combined interdisciplinary unit, students would develop sustainable growing systems in the underutilized New Territories of Hong Kong. They drew out the idea on the back of a napkin!

Where Passion Meets Purpose in Interdisciplinary Experiences

Loni Berqvist, Imagine IF founder and former High Tech project teacher, shares insight around another starting point for these interdisciplinary experiences,

> A lot of the projects that I've done with teachers outside of my subject area have just come from where we have the energy, what are we excited about, and what do we actually want to pursue with kids?

We discussed the sweet spot for co-design a few chapters ago. The same goes for making interdisciplinary connections. The best interdisciplinary experiences lie at the intersection of shared passion and purpose.

What are you excited about? What are your learners excited about? What are current events happening in the world? What teacher shares your enthusiasm for a passion/hobby/ or community cause?

In a Year 9 Social Studies + Language project, student-centered practitioners Mike Strong and Dennis Walker took their shared passion for music, connected it to a community-wide purpose of social justice, and co-developed an interdisciplinary experience around 'Found Sounds from the Underground.' Learners developed their own unique mixed tapes spanning several generations and musical genres, to expose social injustice and spotlight causes and movements to bring about social change. In language, students analyzed songs by influential artists for figurative devices, poetic structures, rhyme schemes, and vocal inflection; while in Social Studies, they studied broader contexts for the music in terms of the political structures, economic inequities, and law-making institutions each song described. The result was 25 unique compilations of music that combined into a Social Justice class playlist.

From Trans-Disciplinary to Working Like Professionals in Interdisciplinary Experiences

The experiences above all moved beyond the transdisciplinary realm of simply connecting learning to an overarching theme or concept, and into the interdisciplinary realm of using newfound understanding to create something meaningful. Students created real, useful products for a real audience. In the process, they had to think, act, work, and produce in a way authentic to the way these disciplines work together in the real world.

Thinking in an interdisciplinary fashion means instead of having students create posters or slide decks to share learning with classmates, they create real products to be shared with the community.

How might you allow for the same authentic dispositions in the interdisciplinary experiences you co-design?

I can understand the initial trepidation. Most of us do not have a lot of experience working as professionals in careers outside of education. I know I don't.

But that's where we can invite experts to work alongside students or share more around their process. If engaging students in small-scale building projects, we can invite architects, engineers, plumbers, surveyors, and real estate speculators to share how their disciplines work together in developing the floor plans, land surveys, and the shell of the home. If engaging students in developing computer games or apps, we can invite computer programmers, software developers, entrepreneurs, designers, manufacturers, and business managers to share how they combine disciplines to generate the plan, prototype, user experience, and method to bring their product to market.

While our learners may not be seasoned professionals in their field, I wonder what we can do to at least get them thinking and acting like them?

How Do You Scaffold Interdisciplinary Learning Experiences?

Verso International School went all in with interdisciplinary learning. They created longer blocks of time to allow for cross-disciplinary connections; flexible, modular environments to allow for simultaneous task completion; and competency-based reporting structures to allow learning designers (teachers) to assess cross-cutting skills.

And while it would be nice to go "all in" like Verso, developing both the experiences and environments that allow for interdisciplinary student-centered experiences, most of us are still confined to teaching within our own four walls. So here's the magic ingredient that will make your interdisciplinary experiences feel even more "real world."

Milestones/Benchmarks.

That's it. It's that simple.

Co-develop three- to-four interdisciplinary milestones/benchmarks students must achieve as a result of the learning experience, and everything else will fall into place. In the case of the interdisciplinary Verso Boarding School experience, milestones included an infographic, proposal, computer generated or 3-D model, and a presentation. In the case of the interdisciplinary Growing Systems Model, milestones included a research summary, virtual co-spaces with narration, and a persuasive pitch.

After negotiating key milestones across relevant subjects, or in partnership with another subject teacher, you can develop your own subject-specific lessons, activities, and experiences to help learners reach them.

Here's a quick visual representation of which elements to co-plan (highlighted in gray):

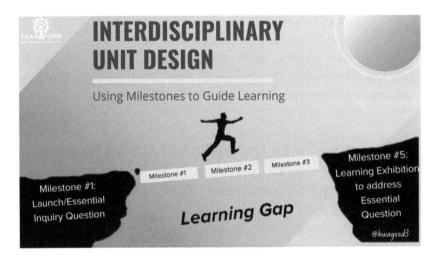

IMAGE 4.2 Interdisciplinary Unit Design Diagram

I can probably predict your next question.

What about Assessment?

How do I assess my subject's learning goals when students are submitting interdisciplinary work? That part isn't as hard as you might think. Identify the relevant interdisciplinary standards and skills required for the milestone and ensure students have been given the opportunity to demonstrate their understanding. If writing a proposal, students can be assessed in languages around the formatting and style of their prose; while in humanities, around the validity and understanding of the content. Students can also be assessed in science around methods of data collection. A single written proposal in this case can be assessed across multiple subject domains.

How do we teach the content? Is there room for direct instruction? Lectures? Traditional teacher-led lessons? Workshops?

Of course.

As mentioned earlier, students will still need our support in developing the skills to reach each milestone. The diagram below demonstrates how you might fill that learning gap.

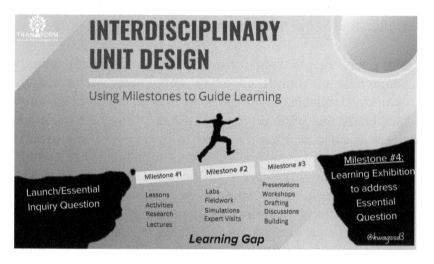

IMAGE 4.3 Complete Interdisciplinary Unit Design Diagram

Visual Created by Kyle Wagner with information adapted from New Tech Network's Project-Based Unit Diagram. https://newtechnetwork.org/resources/what-is-pbl/.

Not ready to devote an extended period of time to interdisciplinary experiences? No sweat. As prefaced earlier, you can choose to sacrifice only a few lessons and support students around a single milestone. That's what Keerapat International School (KPIS) Design Teacher Svetlana Alentyeva chose to do when supporting a Year 5 English Game Design Project. To help learners improve the design of their Language Learning Board games, she gave students a lesson on effective game design. To enhance their physical prototypes, she delivered a lesson on 3-D printing. She also made her space available during break times for students to 3-D print pieces. By restructuring only two design lessons, Mrs. Lana supported several students in transforming into real, professional game designers.

The impact of interdisciplinary learning moves beyond simply preparing students for successive milestones; it prepares them for the kind of meaningful work they will engage with in real life!

Does This Mean I Have to Re-organize My Curriculum? Scoping and Sequencing Interdisciplinary Experiences

Some people fear that organizing learning in an interdisciplinary fashion means a complete overhaul of their current curriculum. It's understandable. I had the same fear as an aspiring interdisciplinary 6th-grade humanities teacher. When the 6th-grade science teacher next door wanted to co-deliver a unit around renewable energy in the first semester, I initially told her it would have to wait until the end of the year. According to my Social Studies Curriculum Map, students didn't learn about citizenship until after gaining the necessary foundations in geography, economics, and civic institutions. But failing to acquiesce to the science teacher's request was not a fault of the curriculum; it was a fault of my own limited thinking. I was viewing my curriculum as a static body of content, rather than a dynamic lens to see the world. Through a simple reframe, I was able to teach these foundational concepts at the same time. While students built their small-scale models of renewable energy next door in science class, in humanities, they participated in a long-term simulation of writing the laws that would bring renewable energy into everyday life. They learned economies of scale, the civic process, and political participation through becoming active members of Congress.

I wonder what opportunities for interdisciplinary connections might open up for you by viewing your content in a more dynamic way? Here's a highly visual and simple starting point: First, share your scope and sequence spreadsheet for the year with your grade-level or cross-department team (Image 4.4). Next, create a tab along the bottom for each year level or subject team to map their own standards/skills according to when they are taught during the year. Once all tabs have been created, look for potential cross-cutting topics, themes, concepts, or projects to integrate the standards around. Do the hard work for your colleagues and find the connections on your own.

Empowering teachers to become architects of learning, where they can map essential outcomes and tailor the learning experience, is the cornerstone of effective education.

This is the strategy Chief Impact Officer Danelle Almaraz uses with schools and districts across the United States to realize blended learning opportunities in their contexts.

Image 4.4 is a sample from Utah:

It's also the strategy the Year 2 Team at Innovations Academy in San Diego to develop its Save our Bees Interdisciplinary Experience; and the Year 5 Team at Cambridge International School in Bratislava used to develop its Healthy Lifestyles Campaign Experience. In helping students develop healthy lifestyle campaigns for peers, teachers across six different subjects infused their mandated curriculum in a meaningful way. See relevant standards/skills' in red in Image 4.5.

As a student-centered leader, how might you use this simple strategy to begin the conversation for interdisciplinary learning in your context?

Building Learner-Centered Environments That Allow for Interdisciplinary Experiences

We've spent a lot of time exploring the mechanics of designing interdisciplinary experiences, but how about interdisciplinary spaces? How do we design student-centered spaces that allow for fluid movement between subjects, and learning goals?

To visualize this environment, we are going to leave school for a minute and take an imaginary trip to my co-working space in Cyberport, Hong Kong, a creative space for tech companies to work, connect, and collaborate.

Upon first entering, you have to adjust your eyes to the bright natural light coming in from the back windows. To your right is a hallway leading to team office spaces, while to your left are individual work spaces shaped like old telephone booths. One person gently closes the accordion doors to his booth and attends to the virtual guest staring back at him through the computer screen. The aroma of fresh coffee grounds and heated bread fills my nostrils as I enter the small, open kitchen. A tenant has just

Essential Learning Map of Claims/Targets and Standards Grades 3–5 English, Spanish, French				
Unit 1: Aug 28 - Oct 10	Unit 2: Oct 11 - Dec 5	Unit 3: Jan 3 - Feb 13	Unit 4: Feb 26 - April 9	Unit 5: April 10 - May 31
Key Details C1/T1 (RL1) identify text evidence (explicit details and/or implicit information) to support a GIVEN inference or conclusion based on the text.	Reasoning & Evidence C1/T4 (RL3, RL6) make an inference about a literary text or texts and identify details within the text or texts that support that inference.	Text Structures & Features C1/T13 (RI5) analyze or interpret why the author structured elements within the text in a certain manner and the impact of that structure on meaning.	Reasoning & Evidence C1/T11 (RI3, RI6) draw a conclusion about an informational text or texts and identify evidence within the text or texts that support that conclusion.	Central Ideas C1/T9 (RI2) summarize key ideas in a text using supporting evidence.
Analysis Within or Across Texts C1/T5 (RL3, RL6) compare and explain the relationships among literary elements (e.g., characters, setting, events) within one text (or across different texts).	Text Structures & Features C1/T6 (RL5) determine how the overall structure of a text impacts its meaning.	Central Ideas C1/T2 (RL2) summarize key ideas and events in a text using supporting evidence.	Word Meaning C1/T10 (RI4/L4b/L4c) use synonyms or antonyms, Greek or Latin roots, or affixes to determine the correct meaning of an unknown word or phrase in an informational text.	Analysis Within or Across Texts C1/T12 (RI3, RI6) determine how information reveals author's point of view across two texts.
Analysis Within or Across Texts C1/T12 (RI3, RI6) interpret how information is presented (e.g., individuals, events, ideas, concepts) within a text.	Word Meanings C1/T3 (RL4/L4a) determine the meaning of a word or phrase based on its context in a literary text.	Language Use C1/T7 (L5a) interpret the intent and use of a literary device in context and analyze its impact on meaning.	Text Structures & Features C1/T6 (RL5) analyze or interpret why the author structured elements within the text in a certain manner and the impact of that structure on meaning.	Edit C2/T9 (L2) Grammar Apply or edit grade-appropriate grammar usage, capitalization, punctuation, and spelling to clarify a message and edit narrative, informational, and opinion texts.
Listen & Interpret C3/T4 (SL2, SL3) identify, summarize, or interpret the purpose, central idea, or key points of a presentation and the use of supporting evidence in a presentation.	Language & Vocabulary C2/T8 (L3a) identify and use the best word(s)/phrase to convey ideas in a text precisely.	Listen & Interpret C3/T4 (SL2, SL3) draw and/or support a conclusion based on content in a presentation.	Use Evidence C4/T4 (W8) select evidence to support opinions, ideas, or analyses based on evidence collected and analyzed.	Revise Brief Text: Informational C2/T3b (W2b) developing and elaborating the focus (main idea) with facts, definitions, concrete details, quotations, or other information/examples

IMAGE 4.4 Scope and Sequence Learning Target ELA Map Years 3–5

Subject	Maths	Science	English	Humanities	Slovak	Art	P.E.	Music
Year 5 Subject Areas	Number, Time, Angles and shape, Calculation, Statistical methods, Fractions, percentages, decimals and proportion, Location and movement, Probability	Models and representations Scientific enquiry: purpose and planning Scientific enquiry: analysis, evaluation and conclusions Structure and function Life processes Ecosystems Materials and their structure Properties of materials Changes to materials Forces and energy Light and sound Electricity and magnetism Planet Earth Cycles on Earth Earth in space Science in Context	Fiction Stories by significant children's writers Traditional tales, myths, legends and fables. Stories from different cultures Non-fiction Non-chronological reports and explanations Unit 2B: Recounts Unit 3B: Persuasive texts Poetry and playscripts Poems by significant poets and playscripts Reading and analysing poems and playscripts and planning and writing them. Narrative poetry Reading and discussing narrative poetry and performing a poem.	Country comparison Comparing and contrasting diets over time and place History of inventions and significant inventors Environmental issues linked with water History of storytelling, theatre and movies	Slovak language around us Slovak geography, Slovak inventors, Slovak curtural personalities, Slovak national parks, Slovak folklore, Slovak traditions	Printmaking, Cityscapes, Adverts	Fitness, Basketball, Net games, Dodgeball, Swimming, Skating, Track and Field, Gymnastics, Invasion Games	Music around the world, differences, traditions, instruments, singing lullabies in different languages

IMAGE 4.5 Learning Target Interdisciplinary Connection Chart

finished heating up her morning breakfast. She sits upright at the neighboring counter scrolling through her phone while taking small bites of her toasted bagel. She is catching up on messages she missed. Just past the open kitchen is a comfortable lounge space with two small coffee tables and colorful couches. A man in khaki shorts and short-sleeve shirt leans back in contemplation, then swiftly moves his fingers across his laptop to type a message. As I move into the large "breakout" room, I peer through the transparent glass to observe an eight-person team huddled around a large table. A digital timeline fills the TV screen that includes dates and short descriptions of relevant activities. A woman with pinned-back hair and a formal blouse stands in front of the screen and, using a laser pointer to highlight each activity. addresses the team seated at the table.

This is not an anomaly. It's a typical Monday morning in an interdisciplinary, co- working space.

How about your classroom? Does it allow for this kind of fluidity between tasks?

While many of us probably lack the funding and licenses necessary to put in movable walls, build small kitchens, purchase multi- functional modular furniture, and mount throw projectors and LCD screens, with a little creativity, we can make our space feel more "co-working" and less "classroom."

- ◆ We can purchase pop up tents and lava lamps at a local garage sale and create a space for focused reading and writing in our classroom corner.
- ◆ Buy cheap, cushioned blocks from IKEA and stack them in the corner of the room. Use them for a quick class huddle, circle time, or open work period.
- ◆ Purchase chalk paint at the local hardware store and transform the pillars in our room into writable surfaces.
- ◆ Get small wood blocks from the local construction site and use them to transform a few of our sitting desks into standing workstations.
- ◆ Cut a large piece of whiteboard into small rectangular pieces and make it accessible in an open cupboard for peer-to-peer teaching.

♦ Get rejected carpet square samples from the home decoration shop and spread them out on the hardwood floor for circle time.

♦ Buy a cheap plug- in stovetop and place it next to your sink for meal sharing.

Trying out even one of the things listed above signals a shift in the power dynamic of our classrooms.

Students will suddenly have increased ownership over their learning environment.

Providing choices over where to work, where to sit, and how to team will also impact how students think and act. By designing spaces that move beyond the traditional bounds of a classroom, we will incite thinking patterns in students that move beyond the traditional bounds of subjects. Walk in at any given time, and we will see students engaged in a divergent mix of activities that transcend siloed subjects, carefully organized according to the needs of the broader learning experience and the learner's personal abilities and interests.

Station-Based Learning

Let's be realistic.

Simply transforming our fixed classroom into one that is more flexible and modular will not change thinking patterns overnight. Remember our leashed dog metaphor from previous chapters? In the same way a dog is first trained on a leash, students are going to need initial guidance in making decisions around what to work on, who they work with, and for how long. One of the best ways to transition learners into taking on this fully autonomous role is to set up guided learning stations. Learning stations are a method of instruction in which small groups of students move through strategically designed centers to learn via hands-on activities.

Elementary teachers at TNS/BeaconHouse Elementary in Lahore, Pakistan, have recently undergone the transition to learning stations (https://tinyurl.com/mua992y8) over the past school year and experienced tremendous success as a result. Walk in during math time, and you will witness students engaged in a number of interdisciplinary math stations designed for them to acquire important concepts. At one station, a small group of students build bar and line graphs out of a given data set to learn how to organize numbers. At another, students build shapes out of small wooden blocks to explore geometric patterns and trans-figurations. At another, students roll a surveyor's wheel across the floor to measure distances and learn how to develop scale drawings. Each station includes a written set of instructions and countdown timer to heighten focus. Some classrooms have even added student station leaders to help guide peers through activities and break down each mathematical concept into child-friendly terms. Station leaders are carefully prepped ahead of time for how to best deliver this instruction.

How about the teacher? What's her role? She takes on the same role she did in shifting to co-design and facilitating inquiry: Her job is to establish the norms, procedures, and protocols to support learners in acting autonomously. Sometimes this means pulling a student aside for a 1:1 conversation. Other times it's jotting down notes of concepts that need to be reinforced in a whole class setting or checking in with station leaders to find out what's working and what needs to change. By the teacher's transition to a facilitator role, learning suddenly shifts from a teacher-centered classroom to a shared, learner-centered community.

How might learning stations help create more interdisciplinary minded, self-guided learners in your classroom?

Building Interdisciplinary Learning Communities

Some schools have invested in constructing the kind of environments that resemble the same co-working conditions described earlier. They are flexible, modular, multimodal, and highly agentic. They reflect the most imaginary co-working spaces of today and the future school spaces of tomorrow.

To witness the power these kinds of interdisciplinary environments have on student agency and thinking, we are going to travel back in time to the launch of an interdisciplinary experience at Yew Chung International School (YCIS) Hong Kong…

It's 8 o'clock on a Monday morning, and 100 Year 10 and 11 students huddle together, eyes glued to a projector screen. Across the screen, a video loops between visuals of huge trucks excreting countless tons of plastic into an overflowing landfill; retail stores packing gobs of clothing garments into large trash bins; and hotel cleaning staff dumping used shampoo and soap bottles into large black trash bags. After pausing the video, the disgust from students was palpable. Chatter erupts amongst them and reverberates off the walls. What was happening? How could their city be so wasteful? After a few minutes their chatter was brought to an abrupt halt by the sound of a deep voice over the house speakers.

"Welcome to the sustainability challenge. As concerned environmental warriors, and ambassadors of HK Youth, your task, if you choose to accept it, is to help Hong Kong create a more sustainable environment. As ambassadors, how can we transform the sustainability of our lifestyle and the communities in which we belong?"

Over the next week, students will work within a flexible, interdisciplinary learning community to fulfill this task.

While the large communal space initially brings the community together to launch the challenge, share ideas, and conduct whole-group activities, smaller "breakout" classroom spaces support small teams in developing their ideas according to the industries they will support. These include Tourism, Fashion, Enterprise, and Marketing. In tourism, students explore how to develop eco-friendly tours; in fashion; how to extend the shelf life of clothes; in enterprise, how to develop environmentally conscious businesses; and in marketing, how to promote more sustainable lifestyles. Two learning facilitators (teachers) host each room and prepare small stations, activities, and hands-on learning opportunities to help students better understand the challenges each industry faces. The entire environment is entirely interdisciplinary and entirely agentic. Students and teachers alike have agency to determine where they would like to spend a bulk of their time learning, and what products they will create.

According to Jill Ackers, learner-centered champion, PBL guru, and a consultant on the learning community design, this kind of learning environment helps provide the three main attributes conducive for active, interdisciplinary learning: "stimulation, naturalness, and individualization."

How might this dynamic, interdisciplinary approach work in your setting?

Collapsing the Timetable to Make Space for Interdisciplinary Experiences

Many schools are answering this question according to their own unique context. Patana International School in Bangkok has committed to collapsing its timetable two times a week for students to engage in interdisciplinary projects around the Sustainable Development Goals. With five rotations scheduled per year, over a three-year span, Year 7–9 students will have engaged in a meaningful, interdisciplinary way with almost all 17 goals. A small interdisciplinary team of teachers will be responsible for designing and facilitating each experience; building connections to the community, curriculum, learners' interests, and projects that help realize each goal on a local level. The hope is that by the end of the interdisciplinary program, students will have developed the skills to design, implement, monitor, assess, and manage projects entirely on their own.

American International School Hong Kong has taken a similar approach to interdisciplinary design. For one week a year, the middle school collapses their timetable for PBL Intensives. These "intensives" are week-long experiences designed by teaching pairs around projects that require interdisciplinary skill sets and thinking patterns to fulfill. Some students combine engineering, physics, and design to build boats to cross the school swimming pool, while others combine art, wellness, and humanities to create murals and culturally sensitive wellness spaces for the school. Since their initial iteration five years ago, the intensives have moved into the greater Hong Kong community, with students taking on interdisciplinary projects that benefit local non-profit community partners. Some students partnered with a refugee organization to bring awareness to the substandard living conditions while others partnered with an organization called Rooftop Republic to co-develop more urban growing spaces. And while each successive iteration might have changed its form, it didn't change its overall goals; helping learners pursue topics based on passion, interest, and real-world need.

Perhaps the most creative approach I have seen to interdisciplinary design comes from ESF South Island School, an international secondary school in the southern tip of Hong Kong. They will collapse the timetable for two days each year to allow students across multiple year levels to address interdisciplinary goals. These goals aren't the brainchild of teachers or local community partners but rather from their own student-led council. Some students will tackle the Sustainability Council's goal of decreasing plastic use, while others will tackle the LGBTQ+ Council's goal of developing more inclusive events and spaces. With the support of adult mentors, each council will co-design a project brief to provide more background around their need, while guiding peers in envisioning a solution. Imagine the momentum an experience like this can build for long-term interdisciplinary, learner-centered experiences. Teachers will gain confidence in transitioning into project facilitators, while students will gain confidence in transitioning into designers, tinkerers, builders, data scientists, and entrepreneurs.

In Closing

What's the easiest way for you to get out of your silo and into the interdisciplinary realm?

We have covered a lot of ground, but there are multiple access points.

Perhaps it's taking a single lesson and connecting it more meaningfully to what students are learning next door. Perhaps it's collaborating on a unit that shares many of the same objectives as a teacher from another subject. Perhaps it's reconfiguring a shared open space to allow for cross-disciplinary activities.

Or perhaps it's designing a more holistic, student-centered learning unit of study.

Remember, to move away from siloed, isolated subject-specific learning and into interdisciplinary experiences, we really need only three main hooks:

A deep, meaningful co-crafted question
An authentic, student-centered outcome
A relevant, interdisciplinary body of content and skills to fill the gap

If we have these three things in place, infusing our mandated curriculum will be a piece of cake.

Take the Scorecard below to identify current practice and target areas for growth:

Shift #4: From Isolated by Discipline to Relevant, interdisciplinary

	Isolated Skills <- ->Relevant, Transdisciplinary					
	1	2	3	4	Now	Next
	Seedling (Sower)	Budding (Builder)	Blossoming (Beacon)	Flourishing (Facilitator)		
Skill Acquisition	Skills are taught in complete isolation, and in individual tasks not connected to deeper learning. Innovative Practitioners work in silos.	Some interdisciplinary collaboration and infusion of content/ skills but not related to deeper learning experiences. Still focused on individual tasks. Assessed according to discrete tasks. While tasks sometimes connect to the overall experience, it is not intentional.	More explicit connection of academic content and "soft"/"hard" skills to overall goals and milestones of units of study, and/or learning experiences. Teachers collaborate to align content and assessments, but do not meet regularly for feedback, reflection and co-planning. Students are assessed discretely rather than having the chance to build on skills for ensuing tasks.	Subjects are used a "lens" to better understand the world." Skills work together in an interdisciplinary way to fulfill the goals and Big Understandings of the learning experience. Curriculum supports the development of milestones. Facilitators work together in a cross-disciplinary fashion at regular intervals to support student acquisition of skills.		

Reflective Questions

1. What step might you take to make learning more inter-disciplinary in your classroom?
2. Who is a teacher you might partner/collaborate with?
3. Where is their overlap in your curriculum? How might skills be merged within a learning experience?
4. What topics, concepts, or Big Ideas might you organize curriculum around?
5. What's most essential in your curriculum? What are a few "power" standards (standards that are most essential for understanding a subject)? What standards might you leave out?

ISOLATED
LEARNING

LEARNING IS
SILOED

SUBJECT SPECIFIC
SKILLS

SINGLE TEACHER
MANAGES

TEACHERS WORK IN
ISOLATION

TEACHERS WO

TE

DISCONNECTED
ASSIGNMENT'S

@ kwagssd3

© 2020 Kyle Wagner and Rob Riordan

TRANSFORM
EDUCATIONAL CONSULTING

IMAGE 4.6 Shift 4 Interdisciplinary Skills Acquisition Infographic

INTERDISCIPLINARY/ TRANSDISCIPLINARY LEARNING

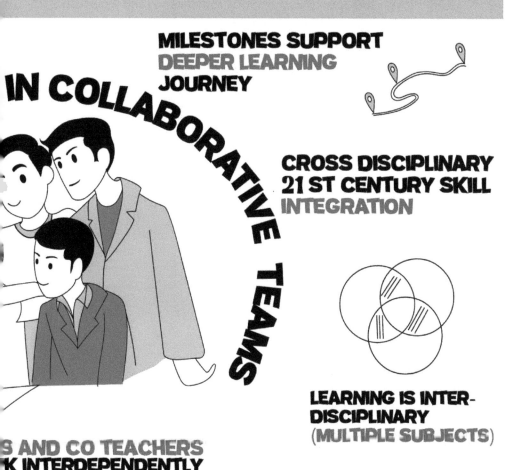

MILESTONES SUPPORT DEEPER LEARNING JOURNEY

IN COLLABORATIVE TEAMS

CROSS DISCIPLINARY 21 ST CENTURY SKILL INTEGRATION

LEARNING IS INTER-DISCIPLINARY (MULTIPLE SUBJECTS)

S AND CO TEACHERS
K INTERDEPENDENTLY

CURRICULAR + COMMUNITY + LEARNING STATION AND SELF GUIDED LEARNING

Bibliography

"These Are the Top 10 Job Skills of Tomorrow – and How Long It Takes to Learn Them." *World Economic Forum*, 21 Oct. 2020, www.weforum.org/agenda/2020/10/top-10-work-skills-of-tomorrow-how-long-it-takes-to-learn-them/

Part II

Curating Beautiful Work and Thoughtful Student Reflection

5

Shift #5: From Limiting Students with Grades to Empowering Them through Pursuit of Their Interests and Real-World Problems

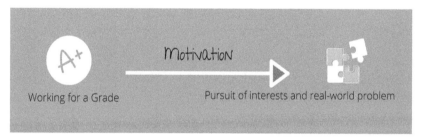

IMAGE 5.1 Shift 5 Increasing Motivation Shift

I think motivation is the same no matter where you teach. And the heart of motivating kids comes from the relationships that you have with kids. And if my number one goal as a teacher is to build positive, solid relationships with kids, make sure that each student feels loved, cared for, safe when they're in my class, and if any of those things aren't being met, there's no amount of motivation you can offer that kid for them to want to do good work for you.

—Mark Shulman, Year 8 Math/Science Teacher
at High Tech Middle School

DOI: 10.4324/9781003398226-8

What motivates you?

I'm sure that answer fluctuates, but I'm willing to bet there are some core ingredients. They're the same ingredients that made you pick up this book: build that extension to your home; achieve dignified honors at your place of work. They are the same ingredients that helped you make new breakthroughs in your field, and work more discernibly and for longer periods of time than you ever have in the past.

And before I tell you what those magic ingredients are, I want you to think back to a project or task in which you had heightened motivation from start to finish. One in which you skipped lunch and worked late hours into the night to complete. A project or task that took more than 50 hours to complete.

For my youngest brother, it was building a detached music studio outside his three-bedroom home. He purchased the shell from a nearby construction store and spent 100-plus hours over three months drywalling, painting, outfitting, decorating, and running electrical to build it to his liking. For my oldest brother, it was building a website design business. He learned a new programming language, devoured countless books, attended blended courses, took interactive tutorials, and built a team. For my middle brother, it was making partner at his law firm. He took on additional trials, stayed after hours to phone prospective clients, and arranged lunch meetings to build relationships with important stakeholders within his firm.

For me, it was creating my first album of music over the course of a summer. After writing the songs, I collaborated with my musician brother to track them at his recording studio. I learned how to use new recording software, create professional audio, lay down instrumental tracks, market on social media, and publish the music via streaming services in the process. For two months I showed up before dawn at my brother's studio and left well after dark.

In all of our long-term projects, there wasn't a supervisor or project manager breathing down my brothers' and my necks. They were self-initiated and self-guided.

According to self-determination theorists, they included the three core ingredients for intrinsic motivation:

Competence
Autonomy
Relatedness

And while there are many more theories among psychologists around what motivates us, they all contain a version of these core components. In Daniel Pink's book *Drive: The Surprising Truth about What Motivates Us*, he calls them "Mastery," "Autonomy," and "Purpose," and contends that when these three components are present, we have the drive to achieve unmatched levels of creativity and productivity in our lives and the workplace. Let's explore these components at work in my brothers' projects.

First, each long-term task required a significant level of competence or mastery to fulfill. Constructing a studio to withstand the elements and allow for professional recordings/production demands competence in craftsmanship and audio engineering. Building a small website design business to attract the right clients and service their needs requires mastery in software development and digital design. Serving high-end clients and winning cases against deep pocketed corporations demands competence in intellectual property cases, and argumentative reasoning.

But projects or tasks that require competence alone will not motivate us. We also need autonomy around the process and outcome. In my brother's studio project, he was able to make his own decisions around the design, specifications, budget, subcontractors, and time parameters. In my brother's website design business, he also got to call most of the shots—the look of his landing page, the clients he would serve, the fee he charged. Finally, in my brother's bid to make partner, he had autonomy in determining which colleagues to connect with, his involvement in each case, and how to best communicate his overall value.

Finally, each project my brother took on was related to a bigger purpose. This "relatedness" helped connect each of my brothers to goals larger than them or than the project itself. My brother's music studio project related to his goal of spending more time with his family, since a detached recording studio meant he could work from home. My brother's design business project related to his goal of creating more flexible time and income, which meant more vacations and evenings with his young daughter. And my brother's becoming partner project related to his goal of helping support more small businesses, since making partner allowed him to have a greater impact.

So how do we take what we know about motivation and apply it to student-centered classrooms?

I can tell you what not to do.

Compartmentalize learning into isolated subjects, with short intervals of time to learn material. This structure is the enemy of *competence*.

Organize learning experiences without the input of learners, with fixed units of study, and fixed reporting mechanisms. This structure is the enemy of *autonomy*.

Make learning a two way conversation between learner and teacher, with nobody to serve or share with. This structure is the enemy of *relatedness*.

These are the structures underpinning so many of our classrooms. But with a little creativity and imagination, we can organize learning in a way that truly captivates and motivates our learners. And here's how one courageous student-centered educator used what we know about motivation to empower an entire community of Year 5 learners.

Dave Strudwick is the former principal and Lead Educator at Real School Budapest, a school that uses project-based experiences to help students "dream and build a beautiful world." And in the winter of 2021, an opportunity to build a better world fell on his lap. Only four days prior, Russia had unilaterally invaded Ukraine. This unprecedented invasion forced thousands of Ukrainians from their homes and into neighboring countries to seek asylum. Hungary was quick to respond. As one of Ukraine's closest neighbors, Budapest offered immediate relief to these displaced families; offering temporary housing, health, education, and basic care. REAL School opened the doors on its campus for a local educational non-profit to run free Saturday School language classes for refugee families. And while Dave and other teachers from his school voluntarily gave up their Saturdays to support in lessons and activities, a new problem surfaced. The charity lacked the resources, personnel, and funding to serve the growing number of refugees .

How would they acquire these much-needed resources?

That's when Dave and his third-to-fifth-grade class got super creative.

Back at school, they were in the midst of exploring a unit around sustainability and fashion; investigating the negative impact fast fashion had on the environment—from its resource depletion in production, to the waste it generated in fast consumption and distribution. And while the learning certainly motivated students, they needed a real community partner to serve in exploration. So what's sustainability and slow fashion got to do with supporting displaced families from Ukraine?

Students would co-create a sustainable fashion show and author a magazine to fund the cause.

Their Big Question: *How can we help our community build a beautiful world?*

Dave's classroom transformed into a fashion company and magazine publishing house overnight.

Students had autonomy in the topics they explored. Some researched and wrote about clothing materials and composition; others, landfills and their impact on the environment; more, around sustainable designs and fast versus slow fashion.

Students also had creative license in the outfits they assembled. Some developed casual wear, while others designed formal wear out of upcycled garments.

In writing the magazine and preparing for the fashion show, they built competence around the same proficiencies as professionals in the real world. They gained these proficiencies by working alongside real-world experts.

To generate their magazine layout, they worked in partnership with a Ukrainian magazine designer/publisher in residence.

To generate their themes—cohesive clothing designs—and appeal to diverse communities, they worked in partnership with an inclusive fashion designer.

To research their sub-topics and effectively publish their short articles, students took mini-workshops on ethical and responsible journalism from a *Guardian* reporter!

To help with their "catwalk prep" for modeling different outfits, students learned effective runway walks from parents who were former fashion models.

To get their makeup looking flawless, students took hands-on lessons from a parent who worked in the film industry.

To help sew their clothes, they learned stitching patterns and techniques from Ukrainian grandparents.

And when the curtains came up on the day of their fashion show event, it wasn't just their class that took a bow.

Other classes put on their own performances. Students who had regular music lessons developed cross-cultural dances to perform with displaced Ukrainian families. The theater class put on plays to celebrate community and culture. The eldest students learned business principles to put together a small market to sell handmade crafts, including friendship bracelets and necklaces.

This eight-week learning experience had real stakes, a real audience, and real learning.

And as serendipitous as it might sound, it is not any more novel than the kind of opportunities you can create for your students when you know the three drivers of motivation:

Competence
Autonomy
Relatedness

What is a current unit you have to teach, and how might you allow for these components?

I witnessed a physics teacher take a forces and motions unit and redesign part of it into a roller-coaster project that allowed students to create and pitch roller-coaster designs to a nearby amusement park. To design the model roller-coasters, students needed mastery level competence in physics, engineering principles, and risk assessment.

I witnessed a language teacher take a narrative writing unit and redesign it into a book-making experience that allowed students to write and publish short stories for younger peers on how to survive adolescence. To write the books, students developed master level competence in story development and the publishing process.

I witnessed a math teacher take a probability unit and redesign part of it into a game night that allowed students to build and run their own probability games for the community. To create the game night, students developed master level competence in probability models and event coordination.

These experiences all tapped into the three core components of motivation. They required a master level of competence to fulfill, allowed learners autonomy in what they created, and related to a purpose that moved beyond the curriculum.

I am confident that as a student-centered practitioner, you can offer your students the same opportunity.

Here are a few questions to help guide you:

> What is a current unit, topic, or concept your students are most passionate about? What do practitioners in the real world do to demonstrate competence in this area? What kind of tasks do they engage in? How might you engage learners in similar tasks? How might you provide choice and autonomy in the projects, tasks, sub-topics, or related activities that students take up?

Eliminating Grades? An Alternative to Grades

It's impossible to write a chapter on motivation without discussing grades.

Do grades really motivate students?

Before we answer this question, let's travel back in time to the late-19th century to observe a well-known experiment run by Ivan Pavlov to measure motivation in his dogs. Pavlov was specifically interested in learning what caused the greatest saliva excretion, since understanding this might provide a window into how to influence their behavior. He placed small test tubes in their mouths to collect saliva samples and provided them with their first stimulus: Dog food. As suspected, their mouths begin to secrete saliva in anticipation of their upcoming meal. Pavlov jotted down the results. But the next day, Pavlov discovered an even greater source of motivation: his assistant. Upon hearing his assistant's footsteps carrying food from next door, Pavlov's dogs secreted an even greater amount of saliva. Pavlov confirmed this theory with the infamous ringing-bell experiment. Without the accompaniment of food, the bell elicited nothing but elevated ears from his dogs, curious as to the source of the noise. But after only a few trials of ringing the bell immediately before feeding time, Pavlov's dogs' tails wagged uncontrollably while their mouths foamed. Pavlov made a breakthrough in the field of motivation. He concluded that he could use external stimulus to condition a response.

One hundred and fifty years later, we are still using external stimuli to condition desired responses in our dogs. My brother uses a spray bottle for his dog, and another friend simply puts her hands behind her back. Her dog immediately stops yapping and perks up knowing a doggie treat is on its way.

So what does Pavlov's experiment got to do with awarding grades in school?

Grades are the external stimuli to condition a desired responses in our learners. "Pay attention to this, it's on the test." "You have to do well on this assignment, your grade depends on it."

In the short run, much like the ringing bell, our learners exhibit the desired response. Out of fear of a low grade, they tune in during lectures, submit assignments on time, and fulfill the necessary requirements. The grades indeed motivate them. But how about long-term? What about the times when we forgot our stack of doggie treats or ringing bell?

Several studies have been conducted on the effect of academic grades on long-term motivation, and the results aren't promising. One study, after measuring the level of motivation of students who received traditional grades compared to those evaluated by a pass/fail mark and narrative feedback, found that there was greater trust, cooperation, and intrinsic autonomous motivation in the latter group. The graded group demonstrated heightened anxiety and avoidance of challenging courses. Another longitudinal study was conducted on students to measure the effect academic grades in Year 6 had on academic achievement in Years 7–9 and ensuing long-term educational attainment. The ungraded group demonstrated significantly higher academic achievement in subsequent years, as well as a higher tendency to finish upper secondary education, whereas graded students demonstrated the opposite. It's worth noting that the highest correlation between ungraded students and positive performance in subsequent years was most prevalent among "lower ability" students.

Some teachers have conducted their own anecdotal studies and experienced similar results.

Gary Heidt, founder of Nova Lab and high school English teacher, decided to go gradeless when he saw that his students were overly stressed and "just checking achievement boxes, climbing each ladder so they could get to the next." He noticed it "wasn't really about learning or things they wanted to do, it was just about reaching the next tick box." Gary replaced tick boxes with a system of ongoing feedback, narrative comments, and peer review. Students would no longer receive grades on intermediary tasks for longer term writing assignments or projects, but rather feedback on how to improve their work for subsequent drafts. They kept track of each draft in dynamic digital portfolios. To manage the process and keep track of individual progress, students used dynamic Kanban boards to mark tasks that were planned, being worked on, or completed. And while Gary explains that it took time to adapt to an ungraded system, the results were incredible. Students sought out feedback for their work on their own, demonstrated significant growth, and in "pitches" could articulate exactly what they were learning in class. Gary retells the story of one former student, now at the top of her class, who wrote a letter that thanked him for "asking for her thoughts, and listening to them." She goes on, "You taught us that everyone is constantly improving. You taught us not like children, but like high-minded people."

How do you currently evaluate student learning? What might happen to your student's intrinsic motivation by decoupling learning from grades? What if you started measuring growth?

You may not have the freedom of going gradeless in your class. You may have a rigid school grading policy to adhere to or high school transcript to slot in your class mark—but I bet you have autonomy in how you get there. Rather than equating learning to an accumulation of points, you can equate it with an articulation of new skills. You can build statements with learners around these new skills and expected learning outcomes, and ask students to collect evidence along the way. If you are in a standards-based school, these statements have already been written for you. Allow the statements to initiate a conversation, rather than a punitive mark. If it's a writing piece, it's a conversation with the learner around the organization, fluency, ideas, or grammar; if it's a scientific experiment, it's around the collection of data, communication of results, or forming of a conclusion. These narrative forms of evaluation may take increased time to implement in the short run, but in the long term, they will lead to motivation in our learners that moves beyond the wals of our classroom.

Heightening our students' intrinsic motivation also means taking the time to build relationships and discover what excites and engages them. Marc Shulman, a former colleague and math/science teacher at High Tech Middle School is a master of relationship building. Before launching any new learning experience, project, or topic, he finds out what excites learners. In this way, he isn't forcing prescriptive curriculum down their throats, but instead illuminating a passion that burns from within. Marc admits finding this internal spark isn't always easy. "Sometimes I pull out every trick, every teacher trick out of my pocket, and you can't get some kids excited about anything." This was precisely the case with one particular student who seemed apathetic to all learning experiences Marc introduced. It wasn't until a fortuitous lunch period that Marc finally made his breakthrough. Marc was busy fiddling with a torch and wire in preparation for the Marble Maze Project he would soon be launching when he noticed Ryan peering in from the window.

"Hey, what's going on? How can I help you?"

Ryan for the first time seemed intrigued. "What are you up to? What are you doing? Can I try?"

Mr. Shulman had to mask his excitement. "Sure, you are more than welcome to." He went on, "This is my first day trying it too. I'm not sure what I'm doing. Can we learn together?"

Marc and Ryan spent the next 30 minutes watching YouTube videos and discussing how to make the Marble Maze work. That thirty minute meeting turned into daily lunch gatherings for the next month as they figured out how to make the overall project work. In the process, Ryan designed AC-powered motors and other mechanisms from scratch, co-wrote the kinetic coasters handbook to introduce the project to Marc's students, and even invited friends to give up their lunches to help.

Ryan transformed from the "apathetic, unmotivated learner" into as Marc puts it, "master helper every student went to if they had a problem."

We all have Ryans in our classrooms. Our Ryans aren't motivated by grades. Mr. Shulman tried rubrics, letter grades, due dates, calls home, and even teaming Ryan with his friends. None of these strategies worked. Instead, Marc waited. "Teachable moments" don't come that often for students like Ryan; but when they do, we have to capitalize on them.

How are you allowing for teachable moments in your classroom? What do you do to build relationships and tap into your student's innate intrinsic motivation?

Here are some ideas for how you might discover it:

→ You could set up a series of activities in your classroom and watch what students gravitate to.
→ You could spend the first few weeks of school playing games with students and make notes about the roles they take on.
→ You could create a short Google Questionnaire to discover student hobbies and interests and keep a dynamic spreadsheet to keep it up to date.
→ You could do what Student-Centered Facilitator Jennifer Villapondo does and spend the first week of school

teaching students how to juggle. As students develop new skills, they can teach their peers.

→ You can have students develop their "ideal day" and share it in a photo montage
→ You can follow their posts on social media
→ You can observe how they spend their time during lunch and snack breaks
→ You can take your class to the park and jot down notes of how they spend their time

The simple truth is that we aren't going to motivate all students 100 percent of the time. And I would be lying if I said that supplementing grades with narrative feedback and building experiences that allow for the three components of motivation—competence, autonomy and relatedness—will be a magic bullet. There will always be students that require a little more time and effort. But that extra time we spend helping learners discover their intrinsic motivation in the short term will pay dividends in the long run. We will build self-motivated learners able to inquire, explore, tinker, and create on their own.

Where Personal Interest Meets Real-World Challenge

We spoke a bit around the three core components of motivation according to self-determination theorists. Do you remember what they were? I will give you a hint; they were the C.A.R. that drove learners to achieve incredible results.

But if the car acronym didn't catch on, I've got an even better one for you that I'm confident you won't forget. P + P = P. Personal Passion + Problem/Purpose = Project. When students can match a personal passion with a real-world problem and purpose, they will have heightened motivation to take on long-term projects.

This is the magical formula that motivates learners in a dynamic after school program in Medford, Massachusetts, called Medford CCSR (Center for Citizenship and Social Responsibility)

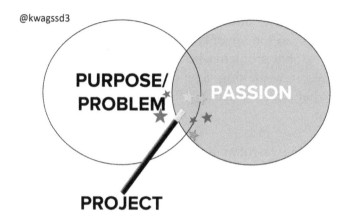

@kwagssd3

IMAGE 5.2 The Three "Ps" Diagram

With the support of adult mentors, students take on real-world problems that include opioid deaths, hatred, prejudice, addiction, bullying, mass murders, climate catastrophes, gender bias, suicide, voting rights, gun control, global warming, pollution, and poverty and address them through meaningful, student-led projects. One artistic high school student, after experiencing merciless teasing around their body weight, worked with the student council and administration to create a "Body Positive" mural in a major thoroughfare of their school. Another engineering-minded elementary student, after witnessing an increase in traffic accidents at a major intersection near their home, worked with the city council to install a 3-D crosswalk. The crosswalk was so effective in decreasing accidents, it was featured on national news for other cities to follow suit. Another social justice minded pair of seven-year-olds, after noticing there were not enough cemeteries for former slaves, worked with the local cemetery to install a slave remembrance stone. It's the first remembrance stone constructed in over 150 years in the area.

Adult mentors support each student in managing their projects by co-creating project timelines, task boards, and shared documents for proposals, presentations, and product development. Older peers also serve as mentors by helping younger peers land on a purpose, project idea, and connect them to the necessary partners and resources to see the project through. At present, it's no longer only a single school working to tackle local and global problems, but an entire community of schools, businesses, law-making agencies, and local representatives. Here's what a former CEO of Teachers 21 had to say about the program:

> What is powerful about how the Center for Citizenship and Social Responsibility operates is that their approach to learning combines lessons in civics, social and emotional learning, and community engagement in a project based framework. Instead of separate initiatives, Rich Trotta and his dedicated teachers have synthesized all the important skills and values we want our students to learn in order to be prepared to improve and strengthen the social fabric that is so critical to our collective well-being.
>
> —John D'Auria

Medford CCSR continues to grow. Every year it increases its number of students, community partners, and adult mentors committed to its cause. And its P3 model continues to motivate.

How might you use the P3 Framework to motivate your learners?

Earlier we discussed ways to discover student passion, but less around finding a purpose or real-world problem to connect it to. You could start with your curriculum. What are some real-world problems that emerge from topics you teach? If it's statistics, perhaps it's using statistics to surface and visualize data around issues that used to live below the surface. If it's chemistry, perhaps it's exposing the chemical compositions of dangerous prescription drugs released by pharmaceutical companies. If it's physical education, perhaps it's using movement to help counteract the obesity epidemic. You could start with causes your students care about. What are injustices they hope to address?

In Closing

The truth is that we aren't going to motivate 100 percent of students 100 percent of the time. And while I have given you some core components, there's no magic bullet. Family circumstances, access to resources, self-efficacy, and diverse learning needs are all factors that are going to affect how much our students care to learn what we have to teach. But we can increase the likelihood that they will care by changing the few things that are within our control. We can provide students multiple opportunities to demonstrate competence; offer increased autonomy and choice in how, what, and where students progress through their learning; build a community for students to share their results with; and help students connect learning to a greater purpose. In the next chapter we will explore how to connect that purpose to real-world work.

Use the scorecard below to rate your current practice of reflection and target specific areas for growth.

Shift #5: Motivation

Working for a Grade< ----------- >Working in Pursuit of Interests and Real-World Problem

	1	2	3	4	Now	Next
	Seedling (Sower)	Budding (Builder)	Blossoming (Beacon)	Flourishing (Facilitator)		
Student Work	Letter Grades drive learning experiences with little to no opportunity for learner to develop and demonstrate competence, make autonomous learning choices, and relate learning to a larger purpose/real-world outcome.	Learning experiences provide some milestones and checkpoints for feedback and for learners to develop and demonstrate competence, make autonomous learning choices, and relate learning to a larger purpose/real-world outcome.	Co-created criteria drive learning experiences with continual feedback offered. Learners have regular opportunities to develop competence, make autonomous choices in learning, and relate learning to a larger purpose/real-world outcome.	Solving a real-world problem while connecting to what learners care about is the driving force behind the learning experiences. Evaluation of learning goals and feedback processes are explicit and criterion based. Learners have ongoing opportunities to develop competence/mastery in reaching goals, making autonomous learning choices, and relating learning to a shared purpose.		

Reflective Questions

1. How do you currently motivate students? What have you learned about motivation from this chapter that you will try in your classroom to increase motivation and engagement?
2. What changes might you make in your current learning experiences to incorporate student's interests, skills, and strengths? How might the 3P model work in your context?
3. How might you connect learning in your classroom to the "real world"?
4. What do you do to foster competence, autonomy, and relatedness in learning experiences? How might you increase it?

LOW-QUALITY, CLASSROOM BASED WORK

EVALUATION
BASED MARKS

SINGLE WORK
SAMPLE

TEACHER-DIRECTED
LEARNING

PURPOSEFUL

LIMITED
CHOICE

TEC

MINIMAL TECH INTEG

FIXED SPACE
FOR WORK

STUDENT WORK
IS HIDDEN

IMAGE 5.3 Shift 5 Increasing Motivation Infographic

GH-QUALITY, REAL-WORLD WORK

MULTIPLE ITERATIONS/ DRAFTS OF STUDENT WORK

STUDIO/MODULAR (FLEXIBLE) SPACES FOR WORK CURATION

INTREGRATED

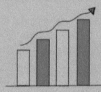

LEARNING PROCESS REFLECTS REAL, DISCIPLINARY WORK

FEEDBACK GROWTH-BASED

OLS

ON

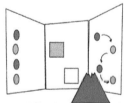

CURATED DISPLAY AREAS FOR STUDENT WORK

HIGH DEGREE OF AUTONOMY, CHOICE

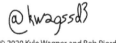

@ kwagssd3

TRANSFORM
EDUCATIONAL CONSULTING

Bibliography

Classical Conditioning - Statpearls - NCBI Bookshelf, www.ncbi.nlm.nih.gov/books/NBK470326/. Accessed 14 Oct. 2023.

Does Grading Affect Educational Attainment? A Longitudinal Study, www.tandfonline.com/doi/full/10.1080/0969594X.2014.988121. Accessed 14 Oct. 2023.

The Impact of Grades on Student Motivation - Cpb-Ap-Se2.Wpmucdn.Com, cpb-ap-se2.wpmucdn.com/portfolios.uwcsea.edu.sg/dist/3/1703/files/2019/10/ChamberlinKelseyGradesQuantitativePaper2018.pdf. Accessed 14 Oct. 2023.

6

Shift #6: From Worksheets and Tests-Based Work to Real-World Products and Services

IMAGE 6.1 Shift 6 Enhancing Student Work

We rush kids through work. They're turning in final assignments every day, 2,030 assignments in a week. It can never be high quality because they're always rushing, and we're always rushing to cover. It's a very different thing that when you think of how in adult life, if you work for an architecture firm or a business firm, you spend weeks preparing a report, and you go over it, and you do draft after draft after draft. Well, what if school were that way? Like, what if school was about producing high quality things?

—Ron Berger

DOI: 10.4324/9781003398226-9

Ten years ago my parents decided to downsize.

It had been over a decade since my brothers and I lived there, and it didn't make sense paying a mortgage on a 3,600-square foot home with four unused bedrooms and 1,800 square feet of unused space. Downsizing would mean more disposable income and less to upkeep. But it also meant getting rid of things they hoped to hold on to forever—pictures, artifacts, posters, memories, and mementos from our bedrooms that reminded them of what it was like to have four kids at home.

Deciding what to throw away and what to keep was too painful. So they left the decision to us.

They armed us with a single storage box each to place any items we wanted to migrate to the new place. These items would be kept in a small attic anytime we wanted to pull them out and get nostalgic about our past. I vividly remember standing in the middle of my beloved childhood bedroom with my empty storage box in hands, wondering how I was going to fit everything I loved into a single, 30-liter container.

I started with pictures. I kept the pictures of my brothers and I performing the "Star-Spangled Banner" at a Major League Baseball game; the signed baseball from the San Diego Padres that I received at birth; my first Gameboy and favorite video games; the newspaper write-up of me winning my first league tennis championship; and rookie baseball cards of my most beloved players. My box was filling up fast.

After several hours of packing and repacking my box, and reminiscing around each childhood memory I kept or left behind, I had space for only two or three more small items. That's when I spotted the large dusty box in the corner of the closet labeled "School Stuff." I was tempted to chuck the whole box. What schoolwork was really worth keeping? But curiosity got the better of me. After opening the box, I pulled out old science worksheets, tests, reports, creative writing pieces around being stranded on a deserted island, and essays on the pros and cons of animal testing. None of it was worth keeping. I threw them all out. There were awards, certificates, and trophies for academic and athletic achievements. I hucked every one of them. I even threw out the ribbon and certificate I received from winning the second-grade spelling bee. I grinned as I recalled my best friend, the runner-up, misspelling a word I knew well.

I was about to give up on the box when I spotted the plastic black spirals protruding from a stack of graded worksheets. When I pulled it out, I knew instantly what it was. It was a scientific report I wrote around using polymers to stimulate plant growth. A plethora of flashbacks flooded my mind as I flipped through the pages. I recalled landing upon my scientific question when my mom told me most of our plants would die that summer because of the drought. I recalled visiting Simpson's Nursery down the street to inquire around how they kept their multiple gardens of plants alive. I remember stumbling upon polymers after chatting with my best friend's mom around how she got her plants looking so healthy. I remember building the planter boxes with my dad to house my experiment. I remember setting up regular intervals during the day to add polymers to the experimental group and check on my control group. I remember building trellises and covering one box with cellophane to test the effectiveness of a greenhouse. I recall creating visual graphs of daily plant growth by hand. My scientific report even included an "acknowledgments" section thanking my mom for "keeping me on track, buying me materials, and for taking me to the library."

I had finally found something from school worth keeping.

But I didn't place that scientific report in the box. I didn't want it to end up collecting dust in my parents' attic. Instead, I placed it in a clear file for safekeeping. As I pen this page of the very book you are reading, that scientific report sits in a file right next to my desk. It helps remind me as an educator to always assign work that is worth keeping.

How about you? What if you could keep only a single piece of work that you completed from your childhood? What would you put in that storage box?

I use this story with educators around the world to illustrate one of my favorite shifts in designing learner-centered environments:

From "Worksheets and test-based work - - - - - - - - - > Real-world inquiry, product or service"

In *Invent to Learn*,[1] Gary Stager calls this kind of work "substantial." It's work that lives beyond the classroom to create a lasting effect. In *Ethic of Excellence*, the legendary Ron Berger calls this kind of work "Craftsmanship." It's work that asks our learners to act, think, and behave like master craftsmen, carefully drafting, re-drafting, and producing products that demand a level of excellence.

Ron shares a vision for what might happen if we engage students in the process of creating high-quality, "craftsman" style work:

> If I want to contribute and build something of quality, then the next step is to ask, what's the genre or format I'm working in. It could be a scientific report, a blueprint, or it could be a physical thing. You're building a model. It could be an engineering design, novel, memoir, or it could be a podcast. What does a professional high-quality one actually look like? What are we aspiring toward— to make a high-quality version of a scientific paper or a landscape design? And so kids, at any age, kids can think, oh, that's what we are aiming for. And then connecting them with people in the professional world who do that work, who are engineers, who are scientists, who are authors, who are politicians, who are engineers, who do that work. When you start working on yours with your students, you bring in experts to critique their work, and the expert isn't a teacher from across the hall, it's the engineer from a firm. Architect. Professional Author. It's somebody who works in the field. Then letting kids go through multiple drafts where their friends are critiquing it, teachers are critiquing it, and outside experts are critiquing it. And finally, polishing that work until it makes a contribution to the world or to their community in some way.

How many opportunities are we creating for students to engage in craftsman-level work?

Let me make one thing abundantly clear. Craftsman-level work ≠ school paint-by-number projects. Creating a hanging mobile of the solar system or the replica of a medieval castle out of toilet paper rolls, cotton balls, and popsicle sticks doesn't ask students to think, act, and behave like real scientists or historians. These artifacts of learning don't make their way into a parent's attic, a museum, or on permanent display in the school office. Rather, most of these projects end up in the Dumpster behind school.

The problem is that most of these Dumpster projects are isolated from the kind of work professionals produce in the real world. Learners aren't ready to build architectural models, publish books, curate exhibits of museums, create radio stations, film documentaries, construct small homes, or publish scientific papers. That kind of work is reserved for graduate students, interns, and career professionals.

But what if it wasn't? What if I told you that every example listed above was work students took on in student-centered environments across primary and secondary school?

In studying communication, marketing, and the changing cultural landscape of Taiwan, learners at VIS Better Lab School in Taiwan created their own radio station.

In studying viable communities, sustainability, and urban systems, learners at Verso International School built an architectural model of a viable future boarding school.

In studying local flora and fauna, biodiversity, and human impact, students at High Tech High wrote and published their own field study.

In studying inclusive environments, elementary school students at Cambridge International School constructed their own playgrounds.

In the age of AI and mass information, we can't afford not to engage students in this kind of work. It's the kind of work that maximizes human potential. Chat GPT can write a five paragraph essay in under 30 seconds, but it can't create authentic products that reflect the collective insights, experiences, and creative ideas of learners.

This chapter explores how we can support students in developing this kind of work.

What Is Beautiful Work?

Asking students to complete craftsman-level work might be a stretch for some of us working in kindergarten classrooms. Aren't we supposed to develop environments that encourage students to take risks? To get away from this idea of perfection and help students become comfortable with the creative process?

Yes—100 percent.

That's why I don't think starting the conversation around meaningful work begins with examining master-level production. I believe the conversation starts by asking students to examine what they find beautiful.

→ That could be in nature: A sunset where bright red bleeds into muted orange as the sun dips below the horizon.
→ It could be a piece of art: A human sculpture with anatomical proportions and muscles so real it looks like it could break free of its marble at any moment.
→ It could be a piece of music: A song that sends electric currents down your spine and spreads goosebumps across your skin.
→ It could be a perfect golf shot: A long iron hit so majestically, the ball seemed to be guided by magnetism to the hole.
→ It could be the setting of a video game level: An alternative metaverse that blends the most majestic of underwater and above-water worlds.

Having a discussion around beauty will open up a larger conversation for the kind of work students might undergo in your class. Inevitably, it will lead to work that extends beyond the blank squares of an exercise book or margins of a teacher-created worksheet, and into the halls of the school and surrounding community.

Matt Neylon, director of Visual and Performing Arts at Mount Vernon, works with teachers and students to curate this kind of work on a regular basis. He contends that, "When engaging in work with students, you have to consider if you are trying to create something that a student finds beautiful, or that a teacher finds good … because oftentimes the answers to those questions are very different."

This is risky territory for a school that is constantly on display. What if the students create something that the teachers don't find beautiful? This happens a lot. When high school students at Mount Vernon worked on an art installation around social justice, they penciled in a mural that featured cartoon-style word art and "graffiti-esque" characters. This was not what teachers were hoping for. Teachers were hoping instead for something that might "hang in the Metropolitan Museum of Art." But when Matt asked individual students what they loved about the installation, they articulated thoughtful reasoning behind each decision: "This piece reminds us of something that we saw under the viaduct as we were driving" or "This piece is actually the same way our favorite athlete writes his name." To the students, this was carefully crafted, beautiful work.

As student-centered practitioners, we are not tasked with getting students to create according to our aesthetic, but to provide them with the opportunity to create according to their own. This doesn't mean we lower our expectations. If students are developing art installations, they should undergo the same process of drafting and revision that real artists undertake in curating their pieces. If publishing field studies, they should take on the same process of data collection that real scientists undergo in organizing and publishing their work. When we expand our definition of beauty, we are able to see that "beautiful work" applies as much to the process of learning as it does the product.

So how do we curate this process?

We design experiences and environments that require students to think, act, and produce according to the lens of the discipline they are studying. If studying the electoral process, students should undergo the same process citizens do in electing their representatives. That's what Kristen Dickey did to transform her fifth-grade classroom during the 2020 presidential elections into an electoral college. Students first decided on class roles and then developed campaigns, wrote speeches, created position papers, and held elections to fill them. And in the same way that members of the electoral college are awarded votes during the election, Kristen awarded neighboring classrooms varying amounts of votes based on their size.

If studying the attributes and lives of heroes, students should undergo the same process anthropologists and biographers do in featuring heroes within their community. That's what Thomas did to transform his third-grade classroom in Bangkok, Thailand, into a publishing house. After examining the lives of famous Thai heroes, students developed interview questions, conducted primary research, and drafted, edited, and published hardcover books that featured heroes within their community.

If studying geometry, students should undergo the same process architects do in designing buildings or outdoor spaces. That's what Marc Shulman did to transform his eighth-grade math/science classroom into a building site. After measuring the area and dimensions for their outdoor play space, students drew up, designed, and constructed the pieces for their unique Gaga Pit. They even presented their concept to school leadership to be awarded funding.

In all of these examples, beautiful work was the result of a curated process of creation. How might you undergo a similar process with your students?

Curating this kind of work doesn't require throwing out what you already have. You could take a series of lessons, unit of study, activity, or learning experience and simply change the outcome to a more authentic product.

You could swap the five-paragraph essay for a class debate.

The research report for a class blog.

The boring PowerPoint presentation for a TED Talk.

The one-off science experiment for a three-lesson field study.

The history paper for a class museum.

Same content with a more authentic outcome and curation process.

Here are more alternatives to traditional products:

◆ Training Manual
◆ Analysis
◆ Field Guide
◆ Speech
◆ YouTube Video Series
◆ Oral Defense
◆ Live NewsCast
◆ PR Campaign
◆ Panel Discussion
◆ Play
◆ Musical Production
◆ Museum
◆ Podcast
◆ Collage/Scrapbook
◆ Video Game
◆ App
◆ Small-Scale Model
◆ Consumer Product

Building Authentic Outcomes according to Your Context

Students desperately want to engage in the curation of beautiful work, especially when it involves the community they care most about.

This was the case for Counseling and Mental Health teacher Barbara Coleman's high school students when COVID hit its peak. The proliferating pandemic and social distancing requirements had taken a toll on their mental and emotional health. Many students felt isolated, disengaged, depressed, anxious, and checked out at school.

Barbara's district scrambled as quickly as it could to provide support, but it was stretched thin. With new COVID restrictions, protocols, and social distancing laws changing on a daily basis, its attention was preoccupied with keeping students physically safe.

And with the counselors' caseload increasing daily, there was simply not enough human power to adequately address students' social and emotional needs. To fill the gap, the district supplied teachers with a social/emotional online curriculum inclusive of lessons, discussion prompts, and ideas for how to stay mentally well. But after only a few lessons, Emily Burk, the district's Makerspace Integration Specialist, confesses that most students were "completely checked out. It didn't meet their immediate needs and did the opposite of what it was intended to do."

Being the adaptive, learner-centered practitioner she is, Emily pivoted and helped Barbara devise an alternative approach. Given her makerspace DIY background, she knew firsthand the benefit students experience when they are actively engaged in learning. She knew the students required something more hands-on. But what exactly would that be? And how might the hands-on learning relate to the specific social and emotional trauma students were experiencing as a result of the pandemic? After attending a district improvement meeting and hearing from behavioral counselors around behaviors they were observing at the lower level, she had her idea: High school students would design therapeutic toys to support the social and emotional well-being of their elementary peers. In the process, they would learn how to best address their own needs. Emily contends, "Having students step away from the computer to focus on the social emotional health of others helps them apply the concepts and reflect upon their own social emotional needs."

The process of curating beautiful work had officially begun. High school students heard from elementary counselors the most pressing needs they were seeing from elementary students during hybrid learning. Through an empathy activity, high school students connected with their younger peers' interests, fears, hopes, and dreams. Next, they defined the specific problems students were facing, and in small teams, began ideating types of therapeutic toys that might provide support for students in addressing each problem. The high school teacher invited behavioral counselors to lead play therapy sessions in the process of ideation and asked for feedback on the types of toys that would most resonate. Next, they rapidly prototyped the solutions. One team built a Superman cape for a student who needed to feel like a superhero to address issues with his self-esteem. One team built a fuzzy, cute monster shaped "worry box" for a girl to dispose of fears and anxiety around what might happen next. In designing each solution, high school students consulted with teachers and school counselors to better understand the background of students and the building blocks of overall social/emotional well-being. Four years later, you can still find those therapy toys in that elementary classroom. And what's more? These authentic products fulfilled the same requirements of the social/emotional curriculum. Students learned how to address social/emotional needs that included belonging, emotional support, autonomy, self-esteem, safety, trust, emotional expression, positive relationships, and self-care. The key difference here: They learned through an *active* process of curation.

Was it beautiful? Absolutely. And not because of the novel and unique therapy toys students created as a result of the learning, but because of the relationships, sense of ownership, and efficacy they experienced along the way.

How about your school community? What are some of its most pressing needs? How might you connect these needs to your curriculum and help students create something beautiful?

Nazeera Khan, after discovering a lack of green space on her campus, led her Year 1 students in creating community gardens. Students learned botany, earth science, and scientific experimentation along the way.

Alexa Leep, after discovering students' apathy toward virtual learning and feelings of isolation during the pandemic, led her Year 5 students in creating a community cookbook. The cookbook shared family recipes and an anthology of family histories behind each creation. Students learned figurative language, narrative writing, and culinary techniques along the way.

Curating each of these experiences required one simple shift:

Moving from worksheets, test-based work - - - - - - - - - - ->
Authentic, real-world product/service

Having trouble thinking up ideas? That's understandable. But remember it's not just you thinking up ideas. Our ideas for authentic products come from a limited repository, but our repository multiplies exponentially when we involve our students.

In the same way students at Mount Vernon thought up the art installation on social justice and Michelle's high school students dreamed up a podcast to redefine the American Dream, you can take your problem/challenge, big question, or curricular topic and brainstorm with them authentic products that might address it.

Here's how to conduct the brainstorm.

1. **Framing the Challenge**: First, frame the challenge, curricular topic, or community need with a driving question. Devise that big inquiry using the same process referenced in the Inquiry Shift Chapter. In Emily's MakerSpace case it was, "How can we as socially/emotionally aware teens best address the social and emotional needs of our younger peers?" In Michelle's literature class case it was, "How can we as GPA authors re-define the American Dream?"

2. **Brainstorming Ideas**: Next, supply students with Post-It notes and pens and ensure tables are grouped together in teams of four. Set the timer for five minutes and let students come up with as many product ideas as they can to address the big question. The main caveat—after jotting each idea down on a Post-It, they must speak out the idea and slam it down on the table. The purpose behind saying it aloud is to help inspire additional ideas from peers. It's the "yes, and" concept: "Yes, we could create a podcast *and* create a blog that goes with it."

3. **Evaluating**: After the five minutes have elapsed, have students separate the Post-Its so all ideas are visible on the table. Next, provide them with a flip chart paper and draw the following quadrants:

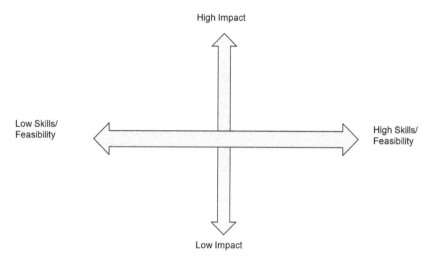

High Impact

Low Skills/
Feasibility

High Skills/
Feasibility

Low Impact

IMAGE 6.2 Project Brainstorm Matrix

Have teams discuss the ideas and place them in the relevant quadrant. For example, designing a personalized AI infused app that supports well-being would most likely have a High Impact, but students might have Low Skills/Feasibility in creating it. That idea would belong in the top left quadrant. You may choose to have students engage in this step silently as students generally get very possessive of their ideas.

4. **Removing/Combining**: After all Post-Its have been placed in their relative quadrants, have students remove any that didn't make it into the top right (High Impact, High Feasibility/Skills). You may also ask them to combine similar ideas.

5. **Share Out**: Next, have each team nominate a team leader to share their high-impact, high-feasibility ideas with the whole class. Write these ideas down on the board.

6. **Advocate**: Next, open the floor for five minutes and allow students to advocate for any ideas they feel strongly in favor of, or opposed to.

7. **Vote**: After time has elapsed, conduct a blind vote with students for the two ideas they like most. Narrow the list down to the two ideas that receive the most votes, and then have students vote again on their favorite.

Congratulations. You have completed the most important step of curating beautiful, meaningful work: Inviting students into the process!

This brainstorming process works for more than just curating authentic products for classwork. You can also use it to come up with a class name, seating arrangement, or topics to study. Just swap out the headers in Step #3 for ones more relevant to the brainstorm you are conducting.

But what if I want to provide students' choice in creating more than one authentic product?

Revolving the class around a few authentic products helps learning feel like a collective process, but if we are to create truly autonomous learners, we need to expand opportunities for product creation. Imagine your entire class undergoing the same challenge or *big* driving question with 25+ authentic products to answer it.

This is what I call Student-Centered Environments 3.0. It's often most successful after students have undergone more structured/guided processes with product curation in 1.0 and 2.0 versions. In guided inquiry processes, it's far easier to ensure multiple opportunities for iteration, feedback, incorporation of real world expertise, and partnership with the community. Once students have undergone the processes of curating beautiful work, they can seek out mentors, resources, and ideas on their own.

But if you are ready to take the plunge into 3.0, student entrepreneurship is one of the best frameworks.

That's the framework Alison Yang, a seasoned learner-centered practitioner, used when engaging an entire secondary school around authentic product creation. Each student was responsible for developing and running their own small business to help fund a community cause. Some students created bracelet businesses, others video game businesses, even more, T-shirt and fashion design. To help facilitate the process, Alison gathered a team of mentors to support students in business development. Mentors included older peers and teachers with relevant experience. With their support as well as process guides, and project-management digital boards, students moved through each stage of iteration;

from conducting market research on campus to pitching ideas for funding and schoolwide selling day at the entrepreneurship fair. In the end, it was more than just the money students raised that turned heads. It was also the way in which students took ownership of the process. They carefully curated a beautiful representation of their own interests, community needs, and entrepreneurial mindsets.

One senior leader remarked, "Bravo to all of you and the students for making the Fair such a huge success. The ambience you created brought upper school parents, teachers, and students together for a positive experience for all."

If you decide to embark on Authentic Product Iteration 3.0, with students creating a number of products in your learning experiences, there are several project management tools and ideas in Chapter 7: "Task Completion: From Isolated to Interdependent and Collaborative."

The Litmus Test for Curating Authentic Products

Whether you are designing with fellow teachers, students, or community partners, I have a very simple and effective litmus test for evaluating the authenticity of product creation. Here are the 4 As to ask:

Appropriate: Is the product appropriate in addressing the main challenge/problem/question/project parameters? Product curation should take into account the built-in parameters of the learning experience. While a comic book might be an appropriate product choice for making Shakespeare accessible for all, it probably isn't the right product choice for greenifying a campus.

Authentic: Is the product authentic? While the form might not be authentic, what students create should be an authentic representation of their unique insights, abilities, and creativity. At American International School Hong Kong, students co-constructed novel soundscapes to enhance different spaces and improve well-being. While soundscapes were not a new concept, the application of soundscapes to their context was authentic in the purpose it served.

Available: Is the product form available in the world outside of school? This question helps us avoid curating products that tend to serve little purpose outside of school—mobiles, dioramas, trifold boards, and PowerPoint presentations. What products do professionals in the real world develop in the process of their learning? That might be a museum exhibit, infographic, phone app, field guide, handbook, or training manual. Our product curation with students should take similar form.

Authentic: Is the product presented to an authentic audience? The products students create should be presented to the audience they were intended for. I can't count how many times I witnessed the showcase of products to parents when they should have been shared with the community. Presenting to authentic audiences means student products receive the feedback, permanence, and usefulness they deserve. (More on how to find and curate these audiences in Chapter 11, "From teacher - - - - - - - > Authentic, public audience.")

You can use this litmus test in tandem with the product ideation brainstorm tool or as a standalone.

Using AI as a Co-pilot in Product Creation

As a songwriter, I always have the idea for a new song in my head. The second the idea comes to my mind, I take out my phone and immediately hum it into my audio recorder. Melodies are as easy as pie for me. Sometimes I even write them in my sleep. What's infinitely harder? Coming up with the right lyrics. That's where AI acts as the perfect co-pilot. A few days ago I asked Chat GPT to come up with the bridge for a song I was writing around two lovers on a road trip. Here's what it came up with:

> *The fire's burning, the stars are bright.*
> *We talk for hours into the night.*
> *The moment's all that we need.*
> *Together, we'll forever be free.*

Together, you and me. [what I wrote]
I brought the bridge to my female accompaniment. She loved it.

When this book is published, I'm not sure if Chat GPT will be as influential as it is now, but it is for sure a game changer in schools. On one side of the coin are educators who view it with trepidation; they fear students will use ChatGPT or other AI tools to cheat; on the other side of the coin are educators who view it with great optimism; they understand the usefulness ChatGPT and other AI tools can provide in learning enhancement.

As student-centered practitioners, I hope we are on the side of optimism.

Cora Yang, a brilliant learner-centered tech coach in Hong Kong, recently helped English teachers enhance their memoir writing unit with animation AI. This tool is able to develop short, animated clips for any piece of writing. Prior to the introduction of this tool, student memoirs were written in longhand and with low rates of engagement; now, with animated videos to accompany their memoirs, students were much more engaged in the learning process.

Other teachers are using AI to support students with ideation, research, reading comprehension, language learning, and skill development. As authentic learning designers and practitioners, we don't have to worry about AI doing our students' work for them. AI can write a five-paragraph essay, but it can't write an individualized memoir based on original research.

Might AI write better? Probably.

Can it draw more realistically? You bet.

Can it solve math problems faster than the smartest brain on planet earth? Of course.

And because it can, it's even more imperative that we design authentic learning experiences with authentic, learner-centered outcomes. In this way, the process of curating beautiful work is more important than the product. (More on process versus product in the next chapter.)

The Use of Real-World Experts in Product Curation

If we want to engage students in authentic product creation, we are going to have to look for support that extends beyond the walls of our classroom. Our expertise goes only so far.

But before we do, take a deep breath and repeat the following phrase:

I don't have to know everything.

Feel better? This is one of the hardest truisms to admit. As the teacher, we have the unrealistic expectation that we should be the omnipotent, all-knowing sage onstage. But the truth is, there are people outside our classroom that know a lot more than us. They possess a unique expertise and real world experience in the fields we generally only teach about. I teach history, but I'm not a historian. You may teach math, but I'm willing to bet you aren't a physicist. If we are hoping for students to think, act, and behave like real professionals in the field, we are going to have to invite them to work alongside.

When our students developed alternative growing systems, they worked alongside real farmers and aquaponics/hydroponics experts.

When developing small businesses, they worked under the guidance of real entrepreneurs.

When publishing books, they worked alongside real publishers and authors.

I know what you might be thinking, I don't have time to go find these experts. I barely have time to think about tomorrow's lesson. But what if I told you that you didn't have to go far to find them? What if I told you there were more than 25 experts who you already knew that were only a quick phone call/email away?

As educators, we all have these experts ready to serve us at a moment's notice.

Our students' parents.

Before launching any new unit, project-based experience, deep dive, or experiential learning opportunity, I send an email to all parents asking for help. I ask for support in adjudication, providing feedback on student work, mentoring project teams, and helping students engage in real world work.

But it's not just me.

It's Linda Amicci, who invited parents who work in city planning to support students in her Re-imagining Westerville Project; Brett Carrier, who invited parents who are food truck owners to judge students' food truck designs; Matt Neylon who partnered with parent car dealership owners to have students co-create PR campaigns; Trevor Shnell, who brought in retired theater directors to support students in creating their class play.

How might your class parents support students in product creation?

I've got an additional hack that usually yields positive results. Have students ask. It's far more difficult to turn a student down than an adult. This is how Nina Jennings found who partners for her class's "adopt a pet" project in Bangkok. Her young learners picked up the phone and rang the non-profits themselves. By the time she launched the experience, she had a local beneficiary ready to partner.

We've discussed several ways to curate and create beautiful, authentic, and meaningful work with students. Now, it's time to home in on a few. I promise your students will surprise you with what they are able to create when they have a meaningful problem to solve. Below is this chapter's scorecard and some questions to help guide you:

Shift #4: Student Work

	Worksheet, Test-Based <----------- >Real World Product, Service, or Inquiry					
	1	2	3	4	Now	Next
	Seedling (Sower)	Budding (Builder)	Blossoming (Beacon)	Flourishing (Facilitator)		
Student Work	Discreet, disconnected worksheets are the basis for learning experiences.	Some interesting activities, lessons, and assignments within learning experience, but are not authentic and student-generated. Student work is "school based" and serves needs of teacher curriculum rather than needs of the learning experience.	Student(s) complete work based on possible real world products or services, but according to teacher designed product/assessment choices. Students have limited opportunities to refine the product or service and share with a community outside of the school or classroom.	In the process of the learning experience, students create a real product/service that serves purpose in the real world outside of school. Facilitator provides multiple opportunities for refinement of the product with expert, peer, self, and community feedback.		

Reflective Questions

1. What piece of work am I most proud of creating in my schooling experience? What made it so memorable?
2. What is beautiful work? How do my students define "beautiful work"?
3. How can I support students in developing work that serves purpose outside of the classroom? What role might parents play?
4. What expertise exists outside of my classroom? From other teachers? Departments in school?
5. What is one place in my curriculum where I can provide more choice to learners around the product?

LOW-QUALITY,CLASSROOM BASED WORK

TEACHER-DIRECTED LEARNING

EVALUATION BASED MARKS

SINGLE WORK SAMPLE

PURPOSEFUL

LIMITED CHOICE

TEC

MINIMAL TECH INTEG

FIXED SPACE FOR WORK

STUDENT WORK IS HIDDEN

IMAGE 6.3 Shift 5 Increasing Motivation Infographic

GH-QUALITY, REAL-WORLD WORK

MULTIPLE ITERATIONS/ DRAFTS OF STUDENT WORK

STUDIO/MODULAR (FLEXIBLE) SPACES FOR WORK CURATION

NTREGRATED

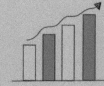

LEARNING PROCESS REFLECTS REAL, DISCIPLINARY WORK

FEEDBACK GROWTH-BASED

OLS

ON

CURATED DISPLAY AREAS FOR STUDENT WORK

HIGH DEGREE OF AUTONOMY, CHOICE

@ kwagssd3

TRANSFORM
EDUCATIONAL CONSULTING

Note

1 See the Chapter Entitled: 'What Makes a Good Project' for the specific reference to substantial work and other components of effective projects.

7

Shift #7: From Product-Based Focus to Process-Based Reflection

IMAGE 7.1 Shift 6: Fostering Student Reflection

> Learning Experiences are like a buffet; reflection is what you decide to put on your plate.
> —Mehak Temur, Learner-Centered Elementary Practitioner, Beaconhouse/TNS

Twenty five university students sit upright in their chairs. Leaning forward, their hands scribble feverishly across blank pages of their journals in an attempt to capture the main points from the quick-speaking presenter in front. "The Kowloon Park Fitness Trail is in desperate need of an upgrade ... and we need your help."

DOI: 10.4324/9781003398226-10

As he shuffles through pictures of fitness equipment at one of Hong Kong's largest parks, he expands on the dilemma. "The fitness trail used to be a bustling place where people of all ages gathered for fitness, play and socializing, but we have seen a significant decline in usership."

He's speaking on behalf of the LCSD (Leisure and Cultural Services Department), an organization that manages most of the outdoor recreation spaces and parks in Hong Kong. He is hoping these university design students can provide suggestions and insights on what kind of fitness trail equipment to purchase that the foreign European playground contractor cannot. Welcome to Week One of the Fitness Trail Redesign Project. After he finishes presenting, student hands shoot up.

"What age group uses the equipment most frequently?"

"What activities are most popular?"

"What time of day experiences the least amount of usership?"

"What kind of recreation are you hoping to see on the trail?"

Students generated these questions with the help of their learner-centered facilitator a few days prior. Through internet research, park maps, and a subject briefing, students were able to home in on exactly what they hoped to learn. And while the presenter is able to provide some general insights, it will be up to students to gain additional insights from actual users in their visit to the park in a few days' time.

They reflect on what they learned and use it to inform their surveys and interview questions.

Week Two

Armed with clipboards, cameras, voice recorders, and their reflective journals, three design students huddle around a short, fair-skinned, dark-haired user between sets at the pullup bars. One team member snaps photos of the pullup bars while the other two find out more about his fitness routine. From their conversation, they learn that he visits the park regularly to do pullups on his lunch break. He wishes the bars weren't so hard to reach.

Another team of students chat with a group of elderly ladies on a nearby bench. They discover that this group visits the park regularly to socialize under the shade of the candlenut trees. They wish there were more shaded areas, and that the fitness trail was more clearly marked. But it wasn't just fitness users that students interviewed. By the end of their field day, students had gathered insights from security guards, maintenance workers, and trail visitors across several age brackets, occupations, and interests.

Back at school a day later, students reflect on their insights and observations. They use giant whiteboards to visually map and categorize these insights according to "problems" and "opportunities." While they concur that fitness equipment is old, uninviting, poorly marked, and lacks diversity, they also agree that there is an opportunity to provide more multi-function use, cross-generational activities, and connection to surrounding nature. Mapping these problems and opportunities helps them converge on the specific concept they hope to design around.

Over the next six weeks, students would undergo a process of ongoing iteration, refinement, and reflection.

When generating creative designs through Mood Boards, students reflected on which designs might be most appealing to young users.

When presenting ideas to a local Playground Supplier Industry, students reflected on which designs were safe.

When co-creating with people with disabilities, students reflected on which designs were most inclusive.

When sharing their re-imagined designs and user insights with LCSD, students reflected on how to fit the designs within the allocated budget.

To help instill this reflective mindset, Alfie Chung, their project supervisor and learner-centered facilitator, never stopped asking questions:

Have you considered the security guards, maintenance workers, cleaners? Who are you really designing for? Are you designing for yourselves or Fitness Trail Users? Who's your real client—LSCD or the park users? What kind of problems are you noticing? What did you learn from your interviews and observations? Is your project following these? How does your design fit with the natural environment? What have we accomplished so far, and what's left to do? Who might we bring in to test your equipment?

Alfie also never clears his whiteboards. "These whiteboards become like artifacts where we keep track of our journey. Every week before we start our lessons, we come in and look at [them]. I ask if their projects are following these; have you forgotten about what you've already done?"

Fast forward to the end of that eight-week journey and envision a team of students standing confidently in front of a rolling TV screen as they summarize each step. Their final presentation is a result of ongoing reflection, from drafting their questions and conducting user research to envisioning, prototyping, and synthesizing their final design.

What does reflection look like in your classroom? Is it something that happens at the end of a unit, project, or set of lessons or something that takes place regularly as part of the learning?

John Dewey once famously remarked, "We don't learn from experience; we learn from reflecting on experience."

Reflection helps cement and etch learning into our long-term memory.

It helps us synthesize findings and apply them to new, novel situations.

It fosters deeper understanding.

But too often in teacher-centered classrooms, reflection is an afterthought—something that would be nice to get to "if there's time."

Ron Berger, who helped to found EL Education and is one of the most reflective practitioners I know, compares the frenetic pace of school to touring countries from a train window:

When my parents shared their European vacation photos with me (14 country tour in 12 days), every picture was framed by a train window. They had been on this train from country to country, taking pictures and stopping for 20 minutes and getting back on the train. And I had this revelation that my entire education was being on that train, with historical dates and mathematical formulas and science formulas and names from literature. And they just went by and by and by. I memorized them for a test and then they were gone. And I thought, what if my parents had gotten off the train in Italy for three or four days and really gotten to spend time, gone to the Uffizi Gallery in Florence and had great Italian meals and learned to understand some of the art and culture, it may have changed them in a profound way. I vowed from that time on, I'm not going to keep my students on the train all the time. We were going to stop sometimes and learn things deeply.

Are you on that same train? Moving from lesson to lesson, chapter to chapter, activity to activity? How might you help get off that train to deepen learning experiences and reflect in the same way Alfie Chung did with his students?

Here are some great tools to help develop us and our students as reflective practitioners.

Interactive Journals/Digital Notebooks

Fifteen years ago, I first discovered interactive journals after watching my mentor run a history class. They were learning about the formation of the US Constitution. They weren't learning to familiarize themselves with random dates, facts, and events, but in order to develop their own class constitution, which would govern how they would act and behave that year. As students learned about key historical figures like Alexander Hamilton, James Madison, and Benjamin Franklin, they reflected on what kind of citizens they wanted to be. The left side of their journals was for jotting down key notes, while the right side was for processing and reflecting on that information. Reflective questions helped guide students. With a collection of notes, observations, original research, preliminary drafts, and other learning artifacts, students were able to visually track their learning. They could go back and reflect on that process.

And when their class constitution was constructed, it wasn't just the authentic collection of rights and responsibilities that was on display; it was the entire process of learning.

Fifteen years later, with the emergence of AI, VR, AR, Google, and laptops, if I were to go back to the classroom, I would still use handwritten journals. And it's not because I'm tech averse. It's because our brains are still wired to connect and process information most rapidly when we put pen to paper.

Cesar Jung-Harada, Founder of Makerbay and one of the most futuristic, innovative, and learner-centered practitioners I know, was invited to a panel discussion put on by StamFord American School here in Hong Kong around the integration of Edtech. Each panelist was asked to share their favorite tech tool and the impact it had on learning. As the microphone was passed, panelist members shared their excitement for VR headsets, the Metaverse, and learning in the Cloud. As each panelist shared, Cesar made sketches in his oversized sketchbook. When the microphone finally reached him, he turned his notebook outward so that the small audience could see, and in his signature, soft and easy voice said, "My journal is my favorite tech tool."

Immediately after the conference ended, I invested in a journal.

How might an interactive notebook build reflective learners in your classroom?

If you need some reflective prompts or activities to get started, you can refer to some of those listed in the inquiry chapters, including "Think, Puzzle, Explore" and "Connect, Extend, Challenge." For a more extensive list of routines for reflection, you can look up Project Zero's from Harvard Graduate School of Education's core thinking routines. There are more than 100 thinking routines that you can easily integrate into deeper learning experiences and use to stimulate student reflection in your interactive notebooks.

If you want to digitize your interactive notebook, I also have a dead easy strategy borrowed from Dominique Hampshire.

Use Google Slides. Make each slide a different prompt, activity or thinking routine relevant to the overall journey of the deeper learning experience. This is what Dom did in her Making Chocolate five week experience. Students were responsible for developing their own chocolate companies and using proceeds from their businesses to benefit a community cause. Their digitized interactive notebook took them step by step through the process of business creation. There were slides on developing survey questions, coming up with a logo/slogan, developing commercials/marketing materials, and deciding on team roles. What's more amazing than the chocolate that most second-graders sold out of within ten minutes of opening their booths? The fact that they were able to articulate their learning journey from start to finish using their digitized notebooks!

Chris Gadbury, a Primary Years Programme (PYP) arts teacher in Hong Kong, has developed highly visual digital inquiry journals for his young learners. The journals include places for student insights, questions, thinking routines, and activities, and frames to support them as they move through inquiry-based experiences.

EdTech powerhouses Tanya Avrith (@TanyaAvrith) and Rebecca Hare (@RLH_Designed) combined forces to construct a beautiful digital process guide called "Reflective Student Curators" for students to work through their own personal passion projects and big questions. There are graphic organizers to support students in coming up with key questions, developing strategies for research, summarizing research findings, coming up with project ideas, seeking out mentors, developing their products, and explaining their findings.

Reflective questions along the way include: What was your goal? What were the criteria? How did you decide to meet it? If you had to do it again, what would you do differently? Any suggestions for other learners taking up similar questions?

What's of less importance than the tool you use are the reflective mindsets you stimulate! You are making a clear statement to learners that you value reflective thinking. Reflection is not just reserved for the end of a learning experience, but regularly along the way.

You don't need to reinvent the wheel in guiding that process. As mentioned in previous chapters, setting up key milestones and checkpoints for your learning experiences ahead of time will ensure students have a roadmap for where they are headed. Their reflections can build upon each other to tell a story of their growth.

You could use already developed processes to help establish those, including the design cycle:

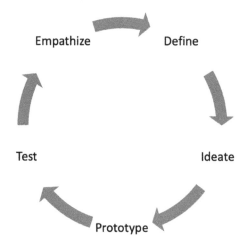

IMAGE 7.2 Design Thinking Process

> **Empathize**: Reflective questions/prompts around understanding specific users' wants and needs that are impacted by the topic/challenge
> **Define**: Reflective questions/prompts to synthesize findings related to user needs and what need to design around
> **Ideate**: Reflective boxes and questions around possible ideas, limitations, and opportunities
> **Prototype**: Reflective questions/prompts around features of the product students develop
> **Test**: Reflective questions/prompts around the feedback provided by users on students' products

Matt Neylon of innovative Mount Vernon School (mentioned earlier) and his team developed an incredibly beautiful Design

Thinking "Playbook" tailor-made for students at his school. Students get to find their superpower, "suit up," develop "adventure grids" for learning more about the problem/challenge and take action through a highly visual "range finder." How might this process be replicated for learning experiences in your context? [1]

If you teach in an Interenational Baccalaureate (IB) school, you might also use Kath Murdoch's Inquiry Cycle to establish milestones for learning experiences and develop reflective prompts:

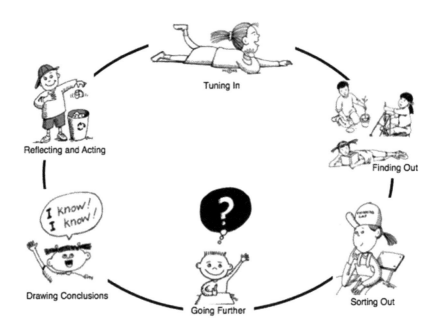

IMAGE 7.3 The Inquiry Cycle

Tbondclegg. "Inquiry Cycle: Why, What and How?" *Making Good Humans*, 13 June 2015, makinggoodhumans.wordpress. com/2015/05/14/inquiry-cycle-why-what-and-how/.

Tuning In: Reflective prompts/questions/activities to tune in to the main topic, concept or challenge

Finding Out: Reflective prompts/questions/activities to explore and research

Sorting Out: Reflective prompts/questions/activities to sort out and categorize research

Going Further: Reflective prompts/questions/activities to dive deeper into a specific project or area of focus students find most captivating

Reflecting and Acting: Reflective prompts/questions/activities around action students take and results they experience

Using an already established, research-based process to guide reflection will help grow the mindsets that allow learners to reflect entirely on their own. In turn, you will be able to step back and become the learner-centered facilitator that is able to reach all students. Fully autonomous student-led reflection 2.0 is detailed below in the form of digital portfolios.

Digital Portfolios/Blogs

Do you remember me telling you about what I experienced when I first walked through the double doors of High Tech High? Not only were students eager to tell me about their school; they were also eager to share more details around each of their learning experiences. The most visual form of this learning was mounted on shelves that lined the hallways and suspended in midair by wires that hung from the ceiling: Shadow boxes with handcrafted student artifacts, wheels connected by hand pedaled gear boxes, murals and art pieces that communicated vibrant stories of their community. But not all student artifacts were three-dimensional. Many of them lived online.

Students took me over to large display monitors that projected their digital portfolios. These carefully constructed, highly visual portfolios demonstrated their journey through learning experiences. They included first, second, and final drafts of learning along with learner reflections. Do you remember Ryan and his marble maze from a previous chapter on motivation? That was there. It included pictures/videos of maze construction and short, narrated video reflections. In one short video he narrates complex physics concepts as his ball moves fluidly through each part of the maze.

Many learner-centered practitioners are using digital portfolios to help learners tell stories of learning. Dagan Bernstein of Hawaii Preparatory Academy dedicates time regularly for his learners to update their digital portfolios with artifacts of work and reflect on their growth through personal Capstone Projects. Jonathan Campbell of Verso International School asks learners to compile video clips into a fluid narration of their journey and growth through IExplore Projects once every trimester.

How might you use digital portfolios to build reflective mindsets in your learners?

You can build frameworks around the digital portfolios that require a minimum number of posts: Posts organized around major milestones, key 21st century skills, or important school values; or posts that respond to reflective questions you and learners have co-developed. The best way to incorporate digital portfolios into your classroom is to just get started!

One of the easiest ways to get started with digital portfolios is through SeeSaw (https://web.seesaw.me/). Students can maintain their own personal digital portfolios in response to reflective questions, assignments, or reflective activities that you share in the main class portfolio. Using a pre-developed platform like Seesaw simplifies portfolio management. As you and your class make digital reflection a regular routine, you can migrate digital portfolios over to more personalizable and autonomous platforms like Google Sites and other portfolio providers. Here are some of my favorites:

- ◆ **Google Sites**: Interfaces nicely with GSuite Schools. Can integrate slide decks, word documents, forms, videos, and various extensions to create a slick-looking portfolio of learning. Pros: Very easy to create and works nicely with Google schools. Cons: Limited access by viewers of the school's domain.
- ◆ **Spinndle** (https://spinndle.com): A customized project management and digital portfolio tool that helps learners monitor and display progress through learning experiences. There are customizable task creators and interactive

comment boxes for teachers to offer feedback as learners progress through project work. Pros: Extremely helpful in managing learning experiences, and making learning feel dynamic. Cons: Not the best visual showcase of student work.

◆ **Unrulr** (https://www.unrulr.com): This one is really nifty. Students upload work and write posts around each stage of the learning experience, and it transforms them into a visual journey of their learning and growth. Students can use this visual timeline during exhibition time (detailed in Chapter 11) to show how they have progressed in aptitude and skills. Many schools are using Unrulr to help students navigate through Capstone or Personal Passion Projects. Pros: Timeline and visual journey tools, can upload to the web and create unique URLs. Cons: There is a cost to purchase a license.

◆ **Wordpress** (https://wordpress.com/) **/Weebly**: This is a completely customizable website/blog hosting site that allows learners to build digital portfolios around their personal preferences. The major advantage of using a website provider like this is the ability for learners to continue building their portfolios after leaving your class. They can use these portfolios to tell dynamic stories of their aptitude/skills to college admission officers, future employers, or new schools. Pros: Personalizable, high degree of learner autonomy, visually appealing, public access. Cons: Higher learning curve, portfolio management, hard to create a uniform look, ensuring digital and cyber safety.

I highly recommend experimenting on the various platforms with your students. Trial each of them in the same way a company would beta test a product before bringing it to the market. I would also invite other classrooms and EdTech coordinators into the conversation as well. This will help instigate a deeper conversation around the importance of regular reflection and student ownership. I have seen many schools implement this strategy successfully with a small pilot group across a number of subjects, year levels ,and divisions. They in turn help onboard other teachers to the frameworks and best practice for portfolio-based learning.

Presentations of Learning

Imagine as a student-centered practitioner if the only thing you provided students through unit based, project-based or inquiry-based experiences was feedback. Much like a graduate adviser supporting their mentees in thesis or doctoral research, you provided timely feedback on learner-developed questions, resources for further investigation, project work, and implementation of different concepts. There were no arbitrary letter grades. Imagine also at the end of their learning journeys, if your students, in the same way graduate students defend their thesis, present their work and new concepts, skills, and insights gained along the way. Imagine them defending their learning with visual artifacts in the form of photos, written work, forms, drafts, and audio bites. This is exactly how students present their learning at High Tech High, VIS Better Lab School, Nova Lab, and other learner-centered environments around the world. Every semester students are required to give a 10–15 minute POL (presentation of learning) to a panel of peers around their learning growth. When they finish, peers ask probing questions to elicit more details. They also provide specific feedback and critique around what the presenter did well as well as potential areas for growth.

Reflective questions help support learners in preparing for their Presentations of Learning.

What are two-to-three new subject-specific concepts you learned?

What were some major challenges you faced in your learning experiences?

How did you overcome them?

How have you grown as a collaborator? Communicator? Creator?

Which pieces of work are you most proud of?

Can you demonstrate how the work developed over time?

What is one piece of advice you would give yourself if you could travel back in time to the beginning of the year?

Tell us about a time you got "stuck." How did you get unstuck? What are one or two academic, social, and emotional/mental goals you have for the next semester?

Single point rubrics help clarify expectations while also supporting the teacher in awarding final marks.

For example: "I can share two relevant, clear, detailed pieces of evidence that demonstrate my growth as a critical thinker ..."

Students at schools with regular presentations of learning think, act, speak, behave, and reflect differently. For them, learning isn't a series of checkboxes and letter grades, but an ongoing conversation and dialogue. When Stacey Duchrow, coordinator of Kenosha School of Technology, visited High Tech High, it wasn't the facilities, projects, or Edtech resources that impressed her the most; it was "students' ability to articulate their learning. I had several students come up to me wanting to share their work, and what they were learning in each of their classes. That doesn't happen at other schools."

And these weren't elementary students, often willing to share learning with anyone willing to bend an ear. These were teenagers. And as anyone who teaches teenagers can attest, you usually get shrugged shoulders, and "nothing," when you ask them what they learned.

Here is a short video put out by students at High Tech High discussing their Presentation of Learning (https://www.youtube.com/watch?v=mW2ABOkejjI&t=27s).

How might presentations of learning build more reflective learners in your classroom?

You don't have to go all in. You could provide a ten-minute window at the end of each class period for students to share and reflect on what they learned. You could invite new students to share or hold the space for any and all reflections. You could support students with a reflective prompt:

"What surprised you about the learning today?"
"What did you used to think, but now know?"

You could trade out mid-unit quizzes or exams with short presentations of learning. Share with students the concepts you hope to assess and ask them to demonstrate competence. Don't have class time for 25 presentations? Have students film themselves demonstrating the concept via ScreenCastify or other screen-recording software and upload to your learning management system or their own digital portfolio.

Most importantly, presentations of learning will help shift the learning narrative from teacher-centered to student-centered. Students will naturally feel more ownership over the learning process when they know they have a choice around how they present it at the end.

Reflective Journey Walls

What fills your classroom walls? I used to fill my classroom walls with pictures of the civilizations and early human species we would study in sixth-grade history. It wasn't until my principal visited my classroom that I realized my error in judgment. While it was nice to have visuals to support the concepts I would teach, she pointed out that there was hardly an inch of space free for student work.

Everything about the way we organize our classroom makes a statement—even the walls. Who owns your classroom walls?

Elementary teachers across KPIS International School in Thailand have begun co-owning their walls with students, and it is having a remarkable impact. They have reserved an entire wall for co-curation of project work. These "journey walls" help share a story of learning that the whole class can reference, reminding them of how far they have come and where they have left to go. For example, Nazeera Khan's wall communicates a journey of school greenification. It depicts students' first surveying of school spaces; drawings of where to place gardens; painting and repurposing of plastic bottles; presentation of ideas to other classes; construction of growing spaces and planter boxes; and brainstorming of accompanying games. Nina Jennings and Carrie Thompson's walls communicate a journey of school waste reduction. It depicts students' initial conversations with cafeteria staff; surveying of neighboring classes; auditing of their own school canteen; conducting hands-on research; formulation of eco-warrior teams; and presentations of waste reduction ideas for an expert panel.

The journey walls help remind students that the process of learning is more important than the product. They are hoping to change mindsets, habits, and interviews around challenges that can't be solved with one simple product-oriented solution. Carrie Thompson, the Year 5 teacher who facilitated the school waste reduction experience, shares:

> My students are now like the waste patrol. They monitor the entire elementary school's paper waste! They won't even let teachers print handouts or worksheets unless it's using recycled paper. If not, they lecture the teacher about it.

This is the kind of "substantial" learning that would make Gary Stager (referenced in earlier chapters) proud. Students are adopting reflective mindsets that live well beyond the expiration date of the project or learning experience.

An alternative to a journey wall in building reflective mindsets is a thinking routine called "Peel the Fruit." In this routine, students make regular visits to a large circular orange in the back of the room to add insights, learning artifacts, photos, wonderings, and questions around a topic, concept, or big question. The orange is a metaphor for the different layers of learning; the outer skin is for observations or noticings; the inside skin is for identifying underlying causes, varying perspectives, connections, and questions; and the core is for articulating the central idea or message.

I have seen this reflective thinking routine work beautifully around concrete topics like Ecosystems, Geometry, and Community, to more abstract concepts like sustainability, justice, and beauty. It helps provide a visual anchor and metaphor for deeper learning and reflection. Similar to a scrapbook, it can be decorated with artifacts as you gather them; quotes from texts you read; pictures from experiments or trips you engage in; statements from interviews students conduct. More on this activity here from Project Zero: pz.harvard.edu/resources/peel-the-fruit.

Personalized Goal Setting with Students

As students move about various self-directed learning stations, student-centered practitioner Mrs. Keri sits down with one excitable sandy-blond- haired Year 6 student at a small table in the corner of the classroom. He clumsily shuffles through a manila folder and pulls out a few pieces of paper while she gently sips a warm cup of lemon tea. One paper depicts a rough sketch of a simple machine he's building with his father; another, a short story he's writing about a shipwrecked group of teenagers stranded on a deserted island. Keri gently prods, "Tell me what you've been working on."

His face lights up. He shares his new discovery of gears and their impact on the movement of his simple machine and the acquisition of new vocabulary to help make his narrative piece of writing more colorful.

Keri smiles and nods in approval. She directs him back to the three goals he established at the beginning of the semester and reminds him of how far he has come.

While we spoke a lot around ways to document and archive ongoing reflection, we didn't speak much around the personalization of reflection. Reflection becomes infinitely more valuable to learners when it is built around specific goals and targets they have identified for growth. In this case, the Year 6 learner established goals around enhancing his creativity and innovation. He targeted specific, actionable areas of building and writing as places where he would implement and collect evidence of his developing skills.

Every student in Keri's class has their own personalized goals and learning plan. The 1:1 conversation I referenced above allows students to reflect and share evidence of the progress they have made in reaching those goals. In true Montessori fashion, Keri does not mandate exactly when these conversations will take place, but instead, asks students to schedule a time to meet with her. "Checking in around Goals" is only one of several self-directed tasks students take ownership in completing. There are other tasks related to subject-specific assignments, key lessons, and project work. Keri has a classroom full of 20-plus self-directed, reflective learners because of the reflective routines she has set up.

How might you allow for personalized, reflective conversations in your classroom?

You might start by having students establish goals. These can be framed around academic, social, and emotional categories, or around 21st century skills/ATLs (Approaches to Learning). I recommend a maximum of three goals per student. Use the S.M.A.R.T. framework to support students in creating actionable plans to achieve the goals. For example:

Goal: "I want to have one piece of my writing professionally published."

Action Plan: Write one-to-two pages every week. Have one peer critique and offer feedback on my writing every two weeks. Purchase a thesaurus and use it to change overused words. Complete a stage in the publishing process once every two weeks (brainstorming, drafting, editing, re-drafting, content/copy editing, publishing).

After setting goals, ask students to schedule times to check in with you around their goals to reflect on their progress. Finally, create a time in the year for students to showcase or present their work and learning (you might make this a part of the Presentations of Learning referenced above).

Making goal setting, reflection, and exhibition a regular part of your classroom environment will help build the kind of reflective learners who are able to take control of all aspects of their learning.

The Art of Reflective Questioning

Twenty-five high school learners stand shoulder to shoulder in a circle around a gigantic wheel imprinted on the ground. The lead facilitator directs their attention to the habits of mind formulating the outer ring. "Curiosity," "'strive for excellence," "empathy" and other attributes enclose the perimeter. He gently asks students to reflect on how they have grown in these areas over their past learning experience.

After time has elapsed, he directs their attention to the inner spokes. Science and Engineering, Arts and Humanities and other core content knowledge and practices enclose each spoke. He asks students to discuss the relevant concepts they have gained as a result of the last learning experience.

Finally, after a few rounds of sharing, he directs students' attention to the inner core competencies. Self-Direction, Social Responsibility, and Cognition. Students share more around how they have grown in these areas.

This kind of reflection is commonplace at Moonshot Academy (https://moonshotacademy.cn/en/), a K–12 school dedicated to "cultivate fulfilled individual, active, and compassionate citizens." The wheel articulates exactly what they are hoping to achieve. Their reflection is timely. I witnessed this particular reflection following a 100 percent learner-led exhibition for the community a day before. Some students exhibited podcasts they created to amplify youth voices while others exhibited the events, panels, and clubs they formulated to address overall well-being.

Their guides embody a reflective posturing. They stand beside learners in the circle; they are an equal contributor to the community.

When was the last time you reflected shoulder to shoulder with learners? Or sat cross legged on the floor next to them?

Posturing ourselves in this way signals to our students that we too are learners. It opens the floor for contributions and insights that carry the same weight and significance as ours. It is in these reflective circles that we are most vulnerable, open, and transparent. Here are ten reflective questions I like to ask:

1. *What surprised you?* Surprise invites mystery and intrigue. It also helps our students look for deeper meaning below the surface of a learning experience.
2. *What's changed for you?* Whether dissecting a provocative piece of literature or reflecting on a collaborative activity or project, this question helps students see how they have grown and changed in the process of learning.
3. *What was your biggest takeaway?* Asking this question helps us discover how to best personalize experiences for learners. We will know which part of the learning experience to keep and what to reconsider for next time.
4. *What challenges did you encounter, and how did you overcome them?* For me, the second part of this question is the most powerful. It's easy for us to get stuck on challenges, but by focusing on our creative solutions, we (and our students) develop new mindsets to deal with future challenges. This question empowers our students to develop resilience.
5. *What was a highlight for you?* This is a much more colorful way of asking, "What did you like most about the last learning experience?" Instead of a bland one word answer, you will have dynamic descriptions that will help you surface what your students really value.
6. *What two or three words would your learning team use to describe you as a teammate?* This is 100 times better than asking a student, "How well did you work with your

team?" It helps them to identify exactly how they contribute while also allowing you to ask follow-up questions to probe deeper.

7. *Which emoticon best describes …?* This question involves some prep work. Print out five to ten emoticons and place them around the room. Ask provocative questions about different parts of the last learning experience. Which emoticon best describes how you feel about our exhibition? *Which emoticon best represents how you feel about your final product?'* Above all, this will help you and your students to see that learning experiences are full of varying emotions, and *all* are ok. They will also help students better recognize their emotions and how it affects their learning.

8. *I used to think, but now I know …* This is a great prompt to help learners identify specifically ways their beliefs, values, or feelings toward learning have changed as a result of a learning experience. It also helps develop flexible mindsets and demonstrate that we are *all* evolving as learners and people.

9. *What was most useful for you?* I borrowed this question from the *Coaching Habit* by Michael Stanier. This question can be used following a learning experience, feedback session, lesson, project, and so forth. More importantly than what your students learn, this question will surface *how* they like to learn. It will help them identify how to best use their time, space, and strengths as self-directed learners in future experiences.

10. *If you could talk to yourself before this learning experience began, what advice would you give him/her?* I adore this question. For your high-achieving students, it will help them be a bit gentler on themselves, and for your lower achieving students, it will help them identify ways to be more self-sufficient in the future. It also avoids the nasty conversation that ensues when you try to give a defensive student advice yourself.

Coming up with provocative questions is only half the battle in building reflective mindsets. Building reflective mindsets and conversations also requires the right protocol to guide it. From my 15-plus years of trial and error with reflective conversations, here is the procedure I would recommend. First, review norms for effective reflection. I suggest co-creating these with your students and could include things like, "one person sharing at a time," "make eye contact with the speaker," "'step up/step back" (based on amount of contribution). Next, choose three-to-five reflective questions to help guide the conversation. I find that ten is too many, and one or two are not enough for learners to truly open up. Write each question separately on a blank piece of paper or on its own slide if projecting the questions to a screen. Project/hold up the first question and ask students to silently reflect on their answer for one minute. After time has elapsed, provide students with three minutes to pair/share with a partner on their left or right. Next, ask for volunteers to share theirs or their partner's insights. (If too personal, the partner can elect not to share.). If there are no volunteers, pull name sticks that you prepared ahead of time. After the student has shared, direct students to offer congratulatory snaps (or silent cheers) to recognize them. Repeat this process for each successive question.

Over time, by creating a safe, non-judgmental environment, students will grow in their ability to reflect. Shyer students will open up; more vocal students will gracefully relinquish the floor; and reflections will deepen in what learners can articulate around new thinking patterns, ideas, or mindsets they have adopted.

Building Academic Language around Effective Reflection

"It was great."

"I liked it."

"It was fun."

Many educators lament that this is the deepest reflection they get from students. I completely understand. It's the same thing I used to get in my sixth-grade classroom 17 years ago. But after careful reflection (like how I did that), my learners weren't the ones to blame. It was my fault for never teaching them the academic language around effective reflection. If we are building utopian civilizations, I should ask students to reflect on their chosen method of food production, means of economic exchange, or procurement of basic resources. Leading with this line of questioning ensures reflection runs deeper than banal phrases.

I would sample with learners how to reflect using this academic language with pre-existing work samples. If reflecting on students' scientific articles, pull up some articles published in academic journals to collectively reflect and critique their study methods, data collection routines, and organization of writing. If reflecting on students' podcast episodes, pull up a reputable podcast episode to collectively reflect and critique their vocal pace, style, and line of questioning. To really cement the expectations around high-quality reflection, co-create sentence starters using the academic language relevant to the experience…

"In regard to intonation, I appreciate …"

"I am struck by how you used an open- ended question to …"

There's a lot more around providing effective critique and feedback in the Chapter 10 shift around Project Assessment, but here's a preview of some great sentence starters for providing feedback that is age, subject, and learning experience agnostic.

"Tell me more about …"

"I'm struck by …"

"I'm confused by …"

"I appreciate the way …"

"I wonder …"

"Your work displays …"

These sentence starters help make the receiver of critique more open to change. Rather than become defensive of their work, opinion, idea, or input on display, they become reflective around how to best ensure it meets the needs of the learning experience, user, or challenge they are addressing.

Let's make one thing abundantly clear: Reflection takes practice. It's not a mindset/skill that we or learners are born with. And if we don't create the space and time for it, we will continue rushing from learning experience to learning experience without actually learning anything. Remember the sage advice from Dewey: "We don't learn from experience. We learn from reflecting on experience"? I have a new favorite quote that came from a student-centered practitioner just like you. "Experience is like a buffet, but reflection is what you put on your plate and take with you." —Mehak Temur, Primary PBL Teacher

What will your students put on their plate when you reflect on learning experiences? After reading this chapter chalk full of strategies, what will you put on yours?

Let's ensure we disembark the school train for long enough to reflect. By creating regular space for reflection, processes to ensure it's meaningful, systems for tracking growth, and artfully constructed questions and language to move beyond the surface, we can ensure our learning trains cover more meaningful ground.

Below is a scorecard to rate your current practice of reflection and target specific areas for growth.

Shift #7: Student Reflection

Reflection on Product < ------------ >Reflection on Process

	Seedling (Sower)	Budding (Builder)	Blossoming (Beacon)	Flourishing (Facilitator)	Now	Next
	1	2	3	4		
Student Work	Little to no opportunities for students to reflect on work, deeper questions, or progress within learning experiences.	Some reflection within learning experiences but not ongoing or meaningful, with few opportunities for personalized student goals and insights driving each reflection.	Regular, ongoing reflection within learning experiences and opportunities for students to reflect on work, growth, and deeper understandings/ questions, but with limited choice for how and where they document their growth.	Innovative Practitioner provides multiple opportunities for students to reflect on work, growth and deeper understandings/ questions with the help of peers, experts, and community members. Students are able to develop personalized goals and create a body of work evidencing progress toward those goals (i.e. portfolios, journals, blogs). Reflection is built into the culture of the classroom and adhered to without teacher prompting.		

Reflective Questions

1. How do you currently have students reflect in your classroom?
2. Is reflection ongoing and continual, or something you do at the end of learning? How might you make more space for it?
3. What tools for reflection shared in this chapter most resonate? How might you adapt them to fit your context?
4. Is goal setting a part of your classroom? How might you support students in targeting and reflecting on personalized learning goals?

REFLECTION ON PRODUCT & PROC[ESS]

CAREFULLY CURATED PORTFOLIOS OF WORK

BALANCE BET[WEEN]

REFLECTIONS ON THINKING, FEELINGS, GROWING , LEARNING

AND INDIVI[DUAL]

REFLECTIVE / PROCESS JOURNALS FOR CONTINUAL REFLECTION

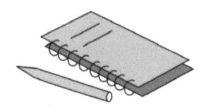

IMAGE 7.4 Shift 7 Fostering Student Reflection Infographic

OPEN ENDED
PROMPTS GUIDE
REFLECTION

N COLLABORATIVE

REFLECTIONS

I USED TO THINK

I NOW KNOW

I GREW AS A LEARNER

MIXED MEDIUMS/
FORMS FOR STUDENT REFLECTION
(WRITTEN, AUDIO, VISUAL)

LEARNING JOURNEY IS
HIGHLY VISIBLE AND
COLLECTIVELLY **CURATED**

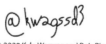

@kwagssd3

TRANSFORM
EDUCATIONAL CONSULTING

Note

1 Resource: https://drive.google.com/file/d/1fpjEnTalvSf9dQid4BX0JH
xpps1EDlvv/view?usp=drive_link

Bibliography

Chris Gadbury et al. "Guided Inquiry Journal for Students." *Toddle Learn*, 22 May 2023, learn.toddleapp.com/resource-post/guided-inquiry-journal-for-students/?utm_source=TeamToddlePost&utm_medium=Twitter_InquiryJournalResource&utm_campaign=InquiryJournalResource

"Peel the Fruit." *Project Zero*, pz.harvard.edu/resources/peel-the-fruit. Accessed 14 Oct. 2023.

"Presentations of Learning: Student Voices." *YouTube*, 26 May 2017, http://www.youtube.com/watch?v=mW2ABOkejjl&t=27s&pp=ygUocHJlc2VudGF0aW9ucyBvZiBsZWFybmluZyBoaWdoIHRlY2ggaGlnaA%3D%3D

Part III

Building a Collaborative Culture

8

Shift #8: From Independent Task Completion to Collaborative Task Completion

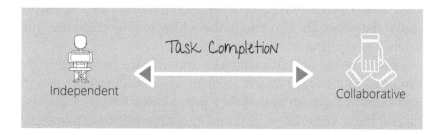

IMAGE 8.1 Shift 8 Supporting Task Completion

We have to focus on collaboration. What does successful collaboration look like? As teachers can we identify that? Can we objectively create criteria that we can see in a group environment? We have to teach kids that. What does it mean to add on to other people's ideas? To not charge ahead and do their own thing? How do you get others to contribute to a group? All those skills that we as adults struggle with often. We have to teach those skills to kids.

—Kristin Damburger, Learning Coach, International
School Nido de Alguilas

DOI: 10.4324/9781003398226-12

The founding members of Lambda Chi were in desperate need of help. Their fraternity numbers were dwindling, most of their funds had dried up, and their fraternity house was a mess. In desperation, they reached out to the five most notorious make-over experts in the world to give their fraternity a makeover. The "Fab Five" got to work immediately.

Bobby, the interior designer and home organization guru, equipped the founding members with mops, toilet brushes, cleaners, cleaning supplies, and a 101 rundown on how to sanitize their fraternity house. He also helped them draw up new room layouts and purchase chic furniture to give the home a new identity.

Tan, the clothing and fashion expert, took the boys to the local fashion mall to purchase new, tailor-made clothes to match their unique personalities. He also helped them upgrade and organize their wardrobe with these new outfits, custom fit for the fraternity outreach events.

Jonathan, the personal hygiene and grooming expert, matched their new clothes with new hairstyles, executed by the barber down the street. He also taught them how to project greater confidence to aspiring fraternity pledgees.

Karamo, the social interaction and culture expert, brought the boys to a nearby beach to open up around deeper stories and sides of themselves that they kept hidden for years. He also helped them formulate norms and agreements for positive social interaction within the fraternity.

Finally, Antoni, food and wine expert, taught the boys how to cook healthy, mouthwatering meals on a shoestring budget. He also helped them work out a meal rotation so that everyone chipped in to feed the fraternity.

Do you know which famous Netflix series I am referencing? It's an episode from the famous series *Queer Eye*.

The Fab Five all had their unique strengths.

They knew their roles.

They also knew how to work together. Their makeovers complemented, rather than clashed with, their peers'. Jonathan's hairstyles complemented Tan's choice of clothes. Bobby's kitchen renovation supported the new meals Antoni taught the boys to cook.

And while they all had individual roles to play, they came together for a common goal: Increasing fraternity membership by elevating the self-esteem and confidence of its founding members.

Contrast this team-based approach with the way we typically run learning experiences in school.

Students complete their assignments and work quietly at their desks.

They are unable to interact with their peers.

Every once in a while, the teacher stops by to check on their progress.

The only way to change tasks is to finish the one they are currently on.

This fixed, independent approach to learning runs entirely contrary to how learning operates in the real world. And it's not just on reality shows like *Queer Eye*.

In law offices, attorneys, paralegals, accountants, and secretaries work in a team-based approach to support clients and prepare for trial.

In home construction companies, architects, engineers, plumbers, electricians, and contractors work in a team-based approach to build homes.

In software development businesses, programmers, developers, administrators, graphic designers, and user experience experts work in a team-based approach to bring new software to the market.

And while teacher-centric classrooms operate in a didactic, one-way direction; in student-centered environments, learning is a dynamic flow between independent and team-based tasks.

Students work in teams to conduct investigations and run experiments.

To complete interdependent project tasks and develop novel products.

To address design challenges, and present unique solutions.

To carry out research and share findings according to their interests and strengths.

That's exactly what learning looks like in student-centered and former Futures Academy facilitator Kristin Damburger's Year 8 classroom. In developing their unique Space Race Companies, students worked in four-person teams to build a custom website, Model Rover, and detailed travel, marketing, and financial plans for how they would carry out planetary exploration.

Completing a project of this enormity would be impossible to take on alone. And in the same way the Fab Five team worked interdependently to help make over the Lambda Chi fraternity, the four-person Space Race Teams would work interdependently to plan their trips to distant planets.

They first matched their individual strengths with project goals using affinity mapping. One teammate would use his/her strength in coding and 3-D design to develop the model Rover, while another would use their strength in graphic design and organizational writing to develop the website. Another teammate would use their strength in mathematical reasoning and physics to calculate the company's financial needs and expeditionary route, while another would use their strength in graphic art to develop the company's logo and marketing materials.

Kristin established protocols and feedback loops for students to receive insight on their project work, from fellow team members to peers and project facilitators. She co-created explicit criteria around each feedback phase so students were aware of the expectations. Kristin also ensured teams were making progress by establishing regular milestones and co-creating a timeline for completion.

As a project facilitator, Kristin observed which concepts students needed extra support with and built mini-lessons around them. In programming their Rovers, Kristin facilitated mini-lessons on various programming commands. In developing their websites, Kristin led mini-lessons on organizational structure and digital literacy. Several of these sessions were led by students.

To help students document individual contributions, reflect on progress, and demonstrate their new understandings, Kristin had students maintain process journals. (Remember these from the previous chapter.) Kristin used these journals as a springboard for 1:1 conversations with students around their strengths and potential areas for growth.

All of these individual check-ins ensured students worked interdependently as a team. When it came time for the final exhibition to potential investors, everyone had a role to play. The science nerd got to articulate the astrophysics behind their company's expedition route; that hands-on programmer got to demonstrate unique functions of the Mars Rover as it roamed the exhibition floor; and that polished presenter got to showcase the long-term return on the company's financials.

Kristin confesses that transforming your classroom from a didactic delivery model to a collaborative, team-based approach is not easy.

> I think there is often a misconception that there is no structure in project-based learning, and that it's just kids fluidly moving toward the completion of a project. But I think as a fellow Project Facilitator we know that it's highly structured. It's just invisible. Everything that we're doing, every move we're making as a teacher is intentional because we know that we have certain goals that we want our students to achieve, and we know what's going to get them there.

But we don't have to run eight-week-long learning experiences like Kristin's to make our classrooms more collaborative. Most of us are not seasoned practitioners, with years of experience creating the invisible structures that allow students to collaborate effectively and seamlessly move from task to task. We can start instead by restructuring a single lesson, activity, experiment, assignment, or learning task to being more collaborative. Rather than ask students to complete the task alone, ask them to complete it in a team.

I witnessed a new student-centered facilitator take this approach with a narrative writing task. Instead of having individual students write their own Greek myths, she allowed students to write in pairs or triads. After brainstorming the concept and narrative arc of the myth as a team, they divided the work in drafting it according to each team member's strengths. One student tackled most of the writing; one, the corresponding illustrations; and one, the historical research to support it. They kept their work in a shared Google Doc to collaborate more seamlessly and so that their teacher could track individual contribution.

I witnessed a new student-centered science facilitator take an independent task around writing a renewable and non-renewable energy report and transform it into a small-group debate. Students formed teams around their favorite form of renewable energy—wind, solar, biomass, geothermal, and hydropower— and then developed arguments around why it was the most viable long-term energy supply. On the day of the debate, teams faced off against each other in multiple rounds. To ensure equal contribution, each team member was responsible for a different round—that is, wind versus solar; wind versus biomass; wind versus geothermal; wind versus hydropower. The science teacher used a five-team round-robin bracket borrowed from the physical education department to organize the tournament.

I witnessed a new student-centered PE teacher take a five-lesson class dance unit and transform it into a small team dance competition. Students formed five-member teams, and through mini-workshops and YouTube videos, learned different dance moves to synthesize into a cohesive routine. More skilled dancers in the group acted as choreographers, while musical students helped coordinate the playlist.

I bet after reading these case studies, you have several ideas for how you might develop a more collaborative, team-based approach to learning in your classroom. But I'm also willing to bet you have even more questions. Here are some of the most common questions I receive from teachers apprehensive about moving to team-based task completion in their classrooms:

1. How should we team students? According to ability level, interest, friends?
2. How do you ensure equal collaboration in teams and delegate tasks?
3. How do you assess learning in teams? Both as a team and individually?
4. How do you manage team conflict and ensure positive communication?

5. How do you determine roles and responsibilities?
6. How do we ensure productivity?
7. How do you handle different working styles and person-alities in teams?
8. How do we help students with time management in teams?

In the next few pages, I will answer each question with tips, tools, and strategies I have seen work best in highly collabora-tive, learner-centered environments.

How Should We Team Students? According to Ability Level/ Skill, Interests, Working Styles, or Friends?

Answering this question leads to a very common conundrum. Team students according to the same ability level, and students might feel more relaxed, but they also could develop fixed mindsets, self-esteem issues, and limited growth. Team accord-ing to working styles, and students might gel well but lack the collective skills to carry out required tasks. Each criterion comes with its advantages and drawbacks. That's why it is best to team students or let them team according to a combination of all five.

I would start like Kristin did with affinity mapping. Develop a list of four-to-five skills required for the task, project, or assign-ment students will take on, and after mapping skills around the room, have students stand under their greatest strengths. I like using affinity mapping as a first step because it affirms that everyone in the class has something to contribute, while often-times overlapping into student interest as well. Next, ask stu-dents to consider their preferred compass point working style/ personality. Are they a big picture thinker, taskmaster, detail stickler, or feelings based collaborator? Having a mixture of these working styles is best for overall team functioning. Have them take the compass test (referenced in a footnote) to deter-mine their style and choose a team accordingly.

Choosing teams isn't an exact science. I would engage stu-dents in several small activities to work in many teams across ability levels, working styles, interests, and friend groups. As students learn more about each of their classmates, they will be more equipped to choose the right team according to the task.

How Do We Teach Collaborative Skills to Students?

As is the case for all skills, kids aren't just going to pick them up through osmosis. If we value collaboration, we have to teach it, and we have to be explicit about what we expect. You might teach these skills by organizing a few fun team design challenges. "Build a spaghetti tower." "Construct a bridge out of these materials that gets this toy car across these two tables." This is how Kristin Damburger built collaborative skills in her students before launching the Space Race Project. At the beginning of the year, students took part in an extensive "boot camp" with a number of design challenges and various teams to work within. After each challenge, Kristin debriefed the collaborative skills that made some teams more successful than others: That is, "we took ideas from all team members" or "we divided up tasks." Learners co-wrote these into proficiency statements using "I can" statements: "We can elicit ideas from all team members." You can do the same in teaching collaborative skills to your learners. As you have students complete each successive team task, revisit, amend, and add to your proficiency statements for collaborative skills. It won't be long before you have a rubric for collaborative skills, with specific examples of each skill in action. (See "assessing" collaborative skills further below for more direction on how to use the rubrics for assessment.)

Or, alternatively you can cheat, and use Chat GPT to generate a list of collaborative skills in less than 30 seconds.

How Do You Ensure Equal Collaboration in Teams and Delegate Tasks?

One of the most common complaints I hear from teachers around group work is that one or two students take up a majority of the work, while the other two ride on their coattails. And while there will always be students who like to take a free ride, I think this problem arises most often because these students don't know how to contribute. The team has not brainstormed roles, generated a list of tasks, and delegated them to the most capable and willing team member. This is most easily accomplished in the short term by modeling this with the whole class using a Scrum Board. A Scrum Board is a dynamic task board that allows teams to monitor progress of tasks toward a shared goal. First, model with students how to create one. Work with students to generate a task list for a hypothetical project/ or learning experience- that could be home building, construction of a garden, creation of an album of music, or the re-design of the school. Write each task on a separate Post-It note (i.e., drawing a plan, hiring a contractor, etc.). Next, allocate students to each task depending on their interest and area of expertise. You can write their initials on the Post-Its. Finally, create a four-column chart with the headings "To do," "Doing/In Progress," "Peer Reviewed," "Done." Place all the task Post-Its in the first column and prioritize from highest to lowest priority. Model moving Post-Its across each column as each task is completed.

With enough repetition, students should be able to conduct this process entirely on their own and effectively delegate and manage group work. This is how Bill Brant and Alex Pilbeam help students manage their self-directed Primary School Community Action and Service (CAS) projects; they allocate tasks after reflecting on their personal strengths and project goals—from school composting to healthy cooking; how Ashley Durdle and Shana Comerford help students manage their Middle School Learning Lab Experiences, from viable city development to play performances; and how Alison Yang helps students self-manage their entrepreneurship projects, from hand-made jewelry businesses to screen printing.

You can set these Scrum Boards up to be either physical or digital. I recommend beginning with physical boards so that you have an easy point of reference for team check-ins. If space is limited, you can create one single board that includes all teams on different rows (with To Do, Doing/InProgress, Peer Reviewed,

Done as column headings). If using digital boards, I recommend setting them up using free programs like Padlet, Trello, or Google JamBoards.

Eventually, students will be able to not only manage tasks, but manage the process of their learning experiences as well. While some teams elicit feedback from their peers, others might be involved in developing a PowerPoint, filming a video, or conducting an experiment. This is what Ros Jackson's "agile" middle school science classroom looked like during a long-term experience where students were tasked with developing an engaging unit for younger peers around rocks and minerals. One pair of students trialed mineralization experiments for the hands-on labs they would develop in the corner; others conducted research around their use in the real world for the unit introduction; others generated lesson plans; and more wrote fun assessments for peers to test their new knowledge. This fluid process was made possible because of the task management systems Ros modeled with her learners.

How might you use Scrum Boards to help students delegate and monitor their task completion?

How Do You Assess Learning in Teams? Both as a Team and Individually?

One of the major reasons teacher-centered practitioners avoid assigning collaborative tasks to students is that they are often very difficult to assess. Do students receive a group grade/mark or individual marks? If they receive individual marks, how do I keep track of what they have individually contributed?

This is certainly a dilemma. Trying to assess 25 individual students across five different teams is going to be next to impossible if going at it alone. But if we empower our learners to be responsible for documenting their own learning journey, assessment becomes far more manageable. In the Space Race Experience, Kristin used process journals and 1:1 check-ins to assess her students. While students worked in teams, they were each responsible for these journals to document their contribution. I also mentioned other tools for self-assessment in the Chapter on Reflection including digital portfolios, interactive notebooks, and presentations of learning.

An even more effective tool is rubrics.

First, when introducing a new learning experience, set of lessons, unit, or project, work with students to identify the skills they will be responsible for demonstrating mastery of. If it's a scientific report, that will include data collection methods, validity of research, conducting of experiments, and so forth. If it's a narrative writing piece, that will include the development of characters, setting, plot, and the like. Develop statements around each skill, pulled from your curricular standards or with the help of Chat GPT. Next, develop a single-point rubric that includes all skills. Laminate it and provide each student or team with a copy. You can keep your own copy in an Excel spreadsheet with separate tabs for each student. Through formative assessments that include journal write-ups, work samples, and 1:1 check-ins, individual students can document progress toward each skill. And while they will have unique team tasks and products they are developing within the team, you can still assess them on their individual progress toward collective learning objectives. There is more on this in the assessment chapter (Chapter 10).

You can also use rubrics to assess students' collaborative skills. How open are they to new ideas and feedback? What's their willingness to compromise? How timely are they on their team-generated deadlines? Can they identify their strengths and contribute in a meaningful way? Generate statements around expectations and try to observe team interaction at least two-to-three times before reporting out. Rather than assess these skills through a letter grade, I would make assessment of collaborative skills narrative and feedback based.

How Do You Manage Team Conflict and Ensure Positive Communication?

Student teams are going to have conflicts. There is no way to avoid it. Sometimes it's around missed deadlines; other times it's around sloppy work; sometimes it's around a bossy team member; other times it's around a team member that seems apathetic. While there is no way to avoid team conflict, there are positive ways to work through it.

First, have teams agree upon clear goals and purposes for their teamwork. A clear goal and purpose will help keep them focused on the bigger picture when conflicts arise. For example, that goal might be, "We are creating a dynamic board game to help our younger peers fall in love with math." Or "We are building green spaces on campus to help improve student well-being, and better connect with nature during the school day." Or "We are creating a play to help show people how to best prepare for a natural disaster."

Next, have teams work together on a contract of expected team behaviors to fulfill that goal. Trevor Snell, a dynamic learner-centered secondary humanities teacher, implemented team contracts beautifully in a class play production. The lighting, sound, set design, script, and production team all had their own unique contracts based on the objectives they hoped to reach and the expected interaction to get there.

Finally, when team conflicts arise, use a dilemma protocol to help teams work through it. Protocols are wonderful in helping get to the root of the conflict; why it's important to address at this time; strategies already implored to resolve it; and the ideal outcome to help move the team forward. I have referenced a framework for this protocol in a footnote,[1] as well as a whole host of other useful protocols put out by the National Reform Faculty (https://nsrfharmony.org/protocols/).

Which of these strategies will you try?

How Do You Determine Roles and Responsibilities?

I discussed earlier the value of affinity mapping in helping teams determine each team member's roles and responsibilities. Again, I would begin by brainstorming as a class the positions necessary to fulfill the project, task, or learning experience objectives. Come up with unique titles. If it's designing learning video games for younger peers, you can have titles like Game Alchemist, Designer of Virtual Realms, Character Creator, Code Conjurer. Work with students to brainstorm the responsibilities each role will take on. Next, have students allocate roles within their team. If there's more than one team member interested in a role, allow them to cross over and share roles.

How Do We Ensure Productivity?

Have you ever given students a long, open-ended assignment or project without establishing checkpoints along the way? I used to. And I wondered why so many students were off-task. Most of the educational world experienced this collective phenomenon when classrooms were forced online during COVID. With full days of time suddenly at students' disposal and only a few check-ins during the day with their classes, many found themselves off-task. Without a teacher within reach to help them chunk time, prioritize assignments, monitor progress, and support when they were stuck, many found themselves drowning in an abyss of too much time and too little understanding of what to do.

But some virtual classrooms flourished.

These were the same classrooms that ran several open-ended projects/assignments, and taught students productivity strategies pre-COVID, when students were in-person. The only thing these virtual classrooms needed to provide was a project overview, an open-ended daily planner, and a few milestones/deadlines for work completion and check-in with peers and the teacher.

It takes time to build this kind of culture of high productivity. Here are some useful tools to begin building it in student teams.

Time Chunks: At the start of a class period, open-ended project work block, or day if you teach in a self-contained classroom, provide students with a simple chart chunked into 30–45 minutes of time. At the top, or in a side column, have them list the tasks they want to complete during the block/ day. Across the top, they can write their major goal. Have them fill in the schedule independently or in a team if they are working on team tasks. Here is a sample planner developed by Instructional Coaches at the International School of Beijing for ELearning:

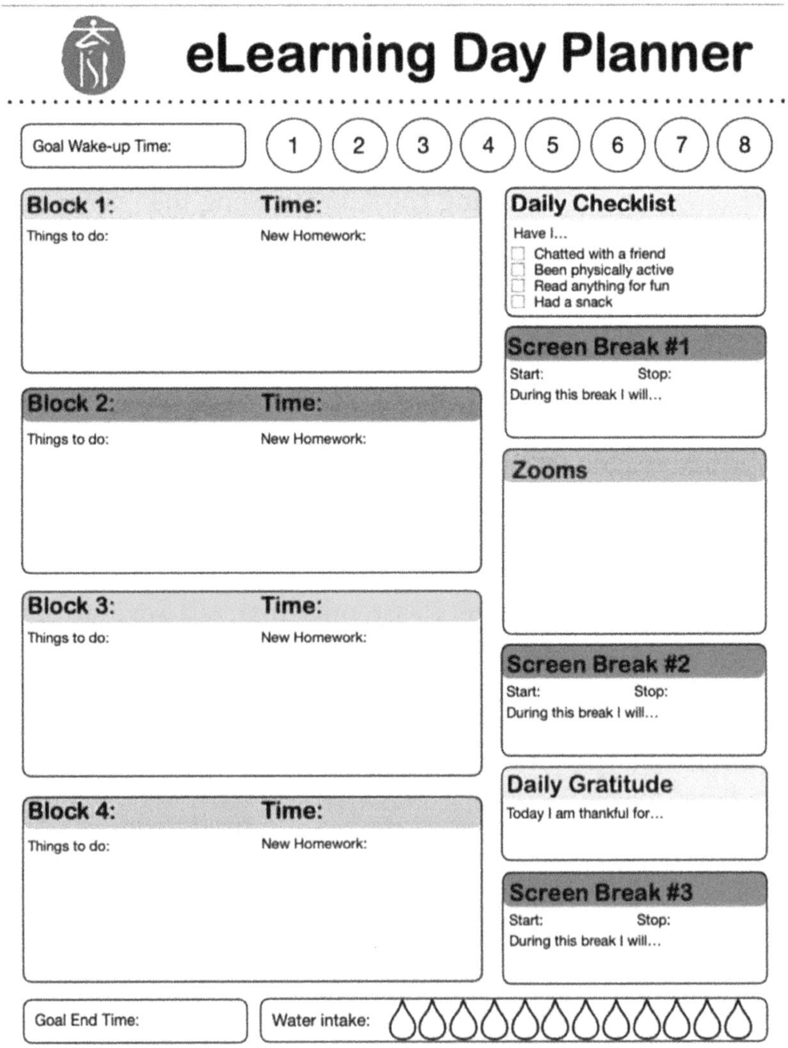

IMAGE 8.2 ELearning Planner

This planner can easily be adapted for group work.

Checklists/Team Folders: Remember our Scrum Board of tasks referenced earlier? At the beginning of open work times, have students prioritize those tasks, and break them down into a checklists of relevant sub-tasks. They can write this checklist onto a blank sheet of paper and staple it to the inside of their "Teams" Folder. At the end of the day/open work time, you can check in with each team to see what they have accomplished and review relevant work samples in their folder. If working in a digital environment, you can use shared digital folders.

Timelines/Due Dates: Prior to teams managing their own deadlines, due dates, and project timelines, I recommend establishing one together. This will keep teams progressing toward the larger goal. This is what Michele Willis did with her podcast project. The class came up with a set of milestones including conducting research, choosing subjects to interview, writing questions, recording interviews, editing interviews, adding music, gaining feedback from peers, writing blog posts, publishing interviews to platforms, exhibiting work. Next, on a free whiteboard she worked with students to develop a timeline of these milestones and corresponding due dates. Much like the "journey walls" we discussed in the previous chapter, students were able to monitor their progress toward each milestone and keep productive. Teams could also work in a more dynamic environment in dividing roles and working more fluidly.

How Do We Manage Workflow and Work Submission in Team Environments?

There's nothing worse than trying to track down assignments from a multitude of teams across a myriad of different platforms. First, I recommend using one central physical digital workspace for work submission and workflow. If physical, you can use the portfolios/team folders referenced earlier. If digital, I have seen some teachers use a combination of Google Docs and Google Classroom. Google Docs is for workflow and process, and Google Classroom for work submission and product. Similarly if using Microsoft, Microsoft Teams can be used for workflow and processes, while pre-created Teams Folders can be used for submitting work. If you and students already work within these platforms, feel free to use them, but if you want to make work submission more public, visual, and dynamic, I recommend using Padlet or Trello. I referenced these tools earlier in regard to task management, but they can also be used for showcasing Team developed products. You simply create "boards" or "padlets," with columns according to project teams. Using a digital visual display space like this allows you to reference high-quality examples, facilitate feedback/public critique, share with parents, and incentivize professional work. Find an example from brilliant Learner-Centered Practitioner Alison Yang here: https://trello.com/b/Zjmh04rE/kis-ideas-2020

What's the Ideal Team Size? Is It Better to Have Teams Work Interdependently on One Class Project or Independently on Their Own?

In my 15 years of experience managing and working with teachers to facilitate teams in student-centered environments, I have seen all sorts of team structuring. I have seen teams of four working independently to propose their designs for a new school playground; and some, interdependently on a collective design for the whole school, with individual teams responsible for different school wings. I have seen students work in small teams to develop their own short documentaries, with each student taking a different role; and I have seen teams work interdependently on a collective class documentary with small teams responsible for each part of production. I have seen five-person student teams put on their own short plays connected to a larger, collective theme; and I have seen classes put on one collective play, with small teams responsible for each scene.

In short, there is no one way to structure teams. Teaming students effectively requires you to consider the needs of the learning experience, the needs and abilities of students, and your experience with dynamic learning/classroom management.

If you are new to student-centered environments, I would suggest creating small teams. Engage the class in addressing one prompt or big question, with small teams determining their unique solutions. Small teams work together on a proposal and product, and then present their ideas. I have used this teaming structure when students designed small businesses, devised unique solutions for the local waterway, and co-authored short novellas.

If you have more experience with student-centered environments and more team-based experiences under your belt, you might try a more dynamic approach with teams working interdependently. I have seen this work with class plays, documentaries, class books/magazines, news teams, and collective events like carnivals. This requires more coordination and inter-team communication but leads to more overall class cohesion.

Whichever structure you decide to use, it's important to keep teams small: Two-to-four students maximum. Keeping teams small ensures increased communication, flexibility, focus, cohesion/connection, and efficient decision making.

How to Foster Effective Communication in Teams? The Team "Huddle"

When team communication breaks down, it's often for a multitude of reasons. Team members aren't aware of their responsibilities; aren't sure what other team members are working on; don't share a common goal; have conflicting ideas; or ways of working.

One way to avoid this conflict is to increase the frequency and structure of communication within your student teams.

Instead of long, drawn-out, vague meetings every few weeks, have teams meet regularly for a focused "team huddle" at the beginning of the day or extended teamwork period. Team huddles are short, 15-minute meetings for teams to celebrate, share updates, address challenges, provide feedback, and coordinate on goals. Here's how to structure them:

♦ **Celebrate Achievements** (two minutes): Acknowledge successes, major milestones, or achievements
♦ **Status Updates** (three minutes): Team members share updates on individual tasks/project work
♦ **Feedback and Collaboration** (three minutes): Team members can provide feedback, seek input, ask questions
♦ **Problem-Solving** (four minutes): Address challenges individual team members or the whole team is facing (could be in regard to resources,
♦ **Coordination on Goals/Priorities** (three minutes): Discuss and agree upon upcoming tasks, deadlines, and priorities. Plan the next steps.

I recommend fishbowling a team huddle a few times with a strong student team before allowing students to conduct in their own teams. Prep the team ahead of time and facilitate the huddle with a visual reference to each step. Debrief with the class and ask them to decide on a team facilitator to guide the process when they meet. This facilitator can also be the team representative when you need to organize a quick "team huddle" with all of the teams. You can huddle with these facilitators and they can relay the message back to their teams.

Team huddles saved my interdisciplinary teaching team from complete collapse during one of our project-based experiences, and I imagine they will carry the same benefit for your teams as well. There's more around team huddles on the internet, and how some of the most innovative companies in the world are using them to help remote and hybrid teams better coordinate and collaborate.

There are probably 100-plus strategies I could introduce to support you in building more collaborative, student-centered team environments, but the best way to learn is to start small. Pick one or two and dive in. You might start with affinity mapping and team folders. Great! Students will have a new way to identify strengths and keep track of teamwork/assignments. You might start with a Trello Team Project Board and Regular Team Huddles. Excellent! Students will have a new way to communicate as a team and a new space to showcase their products. What's even more important than the strategies we employ is the overall outcomes we will achieve. Through our renewed focus on collaborative opportunities, we will equip students with the skills, mindsets, and abilities to lead their own high-functioning teams in the future.

Take the scorecard below to evaluate your current practice in fostering collaboration:

Shift #8: Task Completion

	Independent < --- >Collaborative				
	1	2	3	4	Now	Next
	Seedling (Sower)	Budding (Builder)	Blossoming (Beacon)	Flourishing (Facilitator)		
Task Completion	Students complete tasks independently with little to no connection to others within learning experiences.	Students have a few opportunities to collaborate and complete tasks within learning experiences, but oftentimes without structures, support, or frameworks to guide the collaboration.	Students have opportunities to collaborate within learning experiences, with a few protocols, frameworks and scaffolds to guide the collaborative work. What's missing is regular opportunities to collaborate with outside experts, other teams, and the client or community they intend to serve.	Students have regular opportunities to collaborate interdependently throughout learning experiences within a team, with protocols, frameworks, and scaffolds to guide their work. They collaborate regularly with other teams, experts, and the community they intend to serve. Facilitator creates opportunities and mediums to foster this collaboration.		

Reflective Questions

1. What does effective collaboration mean to you? What would this look like in a student-centered environment?
2. What are one-to two learning opportunities (units, activities, lessons, experiments, projects) that you can make more collaborative or team based?
3. Which challenges listed in this chapter do you often face? What are some tools from the chapter that you will use to help you overcome them?

INDEPENDENT TASKS

SELF AWARENESS OF LEARNING STYLE/ STRENGTH

ENVIRONMENT ALL(
FOR SELF-DIRECTE
LEARNING

SELF-MANAGEMENT OF TIME,'TO DO' ITEMS

FLUID MOVEMENT BETWEEN TASKS, LEARNING STATIONS

CHOICE OF SEATING ACCORDING TO NEEDS

@kwagssd3

© 2020 Kyle Wagner and Rob Riordan

TRANSFORM
EDUCATIONAL CONSULTING

IMAGE 8.3 Shift 8 Independent and Collaborative Task Completion Infographic

COLLABORATIVE TASKS

EQUITABLE TASK DIVISION/ALLOCATION (SCRUM BOARD)

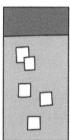

ENDENT TEAMS BASED

N STRENGTH

SHARED DIGITAL SPACES FOR COLLABORATIVE WORK

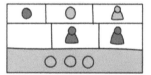

CO-CRAFTED NORMS GUIDE TEAMS

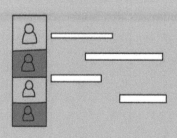

TEAM GENERATED TIMELINE AND MILESTONES FOR COMPLETION

Note

1 https://drive.google.com/file/d/15UvttFZhCtt2vxsjOxigC-bC6vFwuqGn/view?usp=sharing

Bibliography

Compass Points: North, South, East, and West—Statewide System Of …, ilt-maese.weebly.com/uploads/1/0/9/8/109874920/compass_points.pdf. Accessed 14 Oct. 2023.

9

Shift #9: From Teacher-Led Discussion to Facilitated, Socratic Dialogue

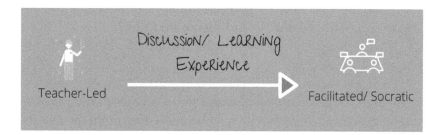

IMAGE 9.1 Shift 9 Fostering Student-Led Discussion

High Tech High is not simply a project-based school; it is a dialogue-based school. We create a culture that allows for good listening and dialogue and honors students' experience as text. Students engage with each other, share with each other their interests, passions, and issues. Through dialogue and collaboration, we aim to overturn the traditional authority relationship between teachers and students.

—Rob Riordan, High Tech High Co-Founder,
President Emeritus Graduate School
(from our podcast interview)

DOI: 10.4324/9781003398226-13

Who holds power in your classroom? How would I know?

This is a question that fascinated me ever since that first fateful day I stepped foot into High Tech High. It was clear that in this school, students held a fair share of the power. They had the power to address adults by their first name. The power to choose their work. The power to devise and research their own questions. The power to organize their schedule and devise their own products. The power to defend their learning and propose a grade.

And it wasn't just High Tech High. I heard about Templestowe College in Australia, where students ran their own electives, held seats on the board, and even managed a portion of the school budget; OneStone Academy in Idaho, where high school students ran their own marketing company, classes and business partnerships with the surrounding community.

I was fascinated with this power dynamic, but equally fearful of what my classroom might turn out to be as a result. Would students quickly become entitled? Disrespectful? Would they transform into the kind of self-righteous brats who smacked gum, put headphones in, and always did their own thing?

I decided to run my own experiment and called it "democratic classrooms."

With the support of High Tech High's Graduate School of Education, I framed a question and for two years participated in ongoing, action research with my classes to document the results. My question: "How do I develop a democratic classroom, and what happens to student engagement and empowerment as a result?"

After looking into a few strategies for implementation, I landed on one I believed would have the most dramatic results: Democratic circles.

Two times a week, I gathered my class in a large democratic circle in the common space outside of my classroom doors. In these democratic circles, students would recognize achievements, lead discussions, address grievances, voice concerns, generate solutions, and make suggestions for future learning and project work. No topic was off limits, and every student had a voice. To create a safe environment and establish a supportive and open culture, I led the first few meetings with students volunteering to take up various parts. It wasn't until the second month of meetings that I decided to give complete control of the meetings to students.

Ahead of their first self-led meeting, they decided on a note-taker, discussion starter, activity leader, and meeting facilitator to oversee the whole process. I removed myself from the circle and took a seat on a bench nearby to observe.

The circle was silent. You could hear a pin drop. I hoped the facilitator would start the conversation by referring to the agenda on the whiteboard, but they didn't utter a word. I hoped the discussion starter would provide a prompt for discussion, but they sat frozen, staring at their feet. I assumed perhaps the activity leader would pull out the cards he brought for the circle game, but he was busy looking at other students.

A fidgety, brown-haired boy finally broke the silence: "What are we doing?"

The student facilitator looked over to me in the corner for directions. I gave him a shrug and a nervous smile. I was determined not to interfere.

Eventually, the democratic circle began, but it was painful to watch. Conversations seemed forced. People spoke out of turn. Students had side conversations. The facilitator didn't adhere to the agenda, and not a single problem was addressed.

After ten minutes, I couldn't take it anymore. I intervened. While embarrassing to admit now, I recall telling them that they weren't ready to lead their own democratic circles. I restored the structure. I ran the rest of the meeting with half-hearted participation. We all felt a sense of failure. I felt I failed them as a learner-centered facilitator; my appointed student leaders felt they failed as peer leaders; and the rest of the students assumed they failed as participants.

Looking back on the incident, I can hear the ghost of Maria Montessori whispering in my ear: "When the child is ready."

I shared my dilemma with my graduate adviser and after listening empathetically, remember her asking one provocative and poignant question.

"Where did you say you were during the meeting?"

I shared that I sat away from the circle, but within sight to ensure a smooth flow. She probed some more. "Do you think you being there affected how the meeting was run?"

My knee-jerk reaction was to assume that students would be even less productive. But after giving it some thought, I understood her point. By sitting within view I was not providing students with the autonomy they needed. In essence, I was still in control.

I met again with my class and told them that I would give them another shot at the democratic circle—except this time, I would be completely removed. I told them that I had a short meeting to attend and would be unable to be there. I would be "in my office if they needed any help." I set up a hidden video camera to record their circle time. (Don't worry, they all signed letters of authorization for pictures and videotaping of my study.)

After students went home that day, I pulled up the recording of circle time and held my breath. The first two minutes were eerily silent, in the same way it was before. But after two minutes something magical happened. The facilitator started the meeting and referred peers to the agenda. The discussion leader had a prompt that elicited sharing from five different students. The activity leader got students interacting, moving around, and collaborating without the circle erupting into chaos. The whole class participated in a brilliant problem-solving discussion around time management during open work time. The note-taker feverishly jotted down notes in the meeting journal to ensure everything was documented. There was a palpable buzz of excitement and purpose.

The video provided a humbling realization: I was not as necessary as I thought. When trusting students and equipping them with some tools to self-manage discussion, I could completely remove myself from the equation. This was the same realization Sugatra Mitra came to when he placed a single computer into a hole in the wall in an Indian slum. Several young children, despite never having seen or touched a computer, taught themselves and peers how to access the internet, develop presentations, create documents, and even create games. Maria Montessori arrived at a similar conclusion when developing her classrooms. With the right environment, setting, materials, and stories, she observed that students were able to work as if "we weren't even there."

How about in your classroom? Could your students still manage if you weren't there?

Building these kinds of Socratic, democratic, student-centered environments doesn't happen overnight. In the same way we worked in the two chapters on inquiry to artfully build a classroom full of curious inquirers, we have to work strategically and patiently to build a classroom full of collegial communicators.

Democratic circles were built on the foundation of several strategies to prompt collegial discussion introduced earlier: Socratic seminars to facilitate deeper discussions into texts; table groupings to facilitate deeper conversations into topics; panel events to facilitate deeper conversations into citizenship; debates to facilitate deeper conversations into varying perspectives. Walk into a student-centered environment that seems to be "owned" by students, and I can promise you it too was predicated on structures, routines, and collegial activities that provided students regular opportunities to assert their voice. This chapter will empower you to reach the same outcome with your learners.

From Squares and Boxes to Circles and Open Space

You can tell a lot about a classroom by observing the way the desks are arranged.

Teacher-centered classrooms all look almost exactly the same. Twenty-five to 30 desks facing the front. The only variation in desk size is the one that seems to be bolted to the floor. You know it's the teacher's desk because there's a permanent name plaque affixed to the top. It's in bold block letters to make sure you don't forget. It's not hard to tell who's in charge in this classroom. Conversations in teacher-centered classrooms are didactic and always originate from the teacher.

Contrast that to a student-centered environment, where no two classrooms look the same. Desks are shaped in unique patterns depending on the learning experience. Sometimes they connect together in a circle to support a large discussion. Sometimes they pull apart into small shapes for 1:1 work and conversation. Sometimes they rise into countertops for quiet, focused work along the back wall. Sometimes there aren't any desks at all. I walked into one learner-centered classroom with 25 cushion blocks and small, foldable breakfast trays. Most learner-centered classrooms don't even have a "teacher desk." If there is a teacher's desk, oftentimes it only takes up a small space in the corner.

And while student-centered environments may differ in appearance, one thing is constant: Power is shared.

How have you arranged the desks in your classroom to allow for shared power? One of the easiest ways to foster Socratic discussion and collegial conversation is to create table groups. Take four seats that used to all face forward in rows and move them together into a small group. Place a box of supplies in the middle and watch the way interaction changes.

Our hope is that discussion will move from being didactic and two-directional to pluralistic and multi-directional.

As a facilitator, you can ensure the right protocols and norms are in place to foster it. Guide each group in developing table group norms around how they will interact, make decisions, speak and listen, utilize each other's strengths, and take notes. You can help by modeling.

Organizing desks into table groups was one of the first ways I moved from teacher-centered to facilitated, student-led discussions within my own classroom. To help model at the beginning, I facilitated the discussions around open-ended, debatable questions based around the content—that is, Is legalism an effective way to govern? Table groups discussed for an allotted amount of time, and the group facilitator would share their insights. I would jot down general themes that emerged on the front board and use it for hooking students into new content. After students became comfortable with facilitating, recording notes, and summarizing their ideas for the class, we progressed into more dynamic, student-led discussions, allowing me to act as an observer. These types of discussions are detailed below.

World Café Dialogue

Imagine your students moving fluidly from table to table group to gather collective insights and respond to student-generated questions and ideas. This is what student-centered environments look like when using World Café. To set it up, prepare your room in the same way you would a café: With light, calming background music and tables set up in small groups throughout the space. Next, choose a thought-provoking topic related to student interest, the community, or the curriculum—preferably one you have already spent time discussing. Give students time within their small group to generate one key question related to the topic to discuss on a deeper level. After developing and writing the question on large butcher paper, students can jot down insights and answers on sticky notes within the small group. When finished, have students appoint a "table host" to welcome new groups and rotate clockwise to a new table to repeat the process. By the end of the activity, you will have a room full of artifacts evidencing deep, student-led discussion.

This jigsaw or "world café' activity can be used to discuss questions, introduce new concepts, respond to prompts, or have peer experts to share learning. Most importantly, it will provide students with an active opportunity to lead their own discussions.

How might a world café work in your context?

Using Socratic Seminars to Dive Deeper

Socrates was one of the most well-known student-centered practitioners of Western Civilization. He developed a famous method for answering every student question with a better question of his own. Ask him why all objects fall to the ground and he might ask why bubbles rise to the surface. His Socratic method was used to explore complex ideas, concepts, and beliefs by asking questions that challenge assumptions, clarify meanings, and reveal underlying principles. And while I imagine this method often drove his pupils mad, I also imagine it helped them start thinking for themselves.

Ultimately, we want to do the same for our students. We can do Socrates proud by progressing from jigsaw and world café discussions into student-facilitated Socratic Seminars. This discussion format allows learners to develop their own questions in response to a text, short story, piece of literature, video, set of illustrations, primary source material, letter, or any significant material that stimulates thinking. To prepare, learners spend time engaging with the learning material—annotating it, digesting its main points, and most importantly, devising two questions for discussion. I often ask learners to develop an evaluative and interpretive question for discussion (see the previous chapter on inquiry for explanation). For example, during our extended unit around food growing systems of the future, students developed questions around a pro-vocative article entitled, "The Pleasure of Eating." We also used *Omnivore's Dilemma* as an anchor text for many discussions.

On Seminar Day, students bring their copy of the anchor learning material, their annotations, and questions for the group. As facilitator, you arrange the chairs into two giant concentric circles. Place half of the students into the inner circle, and half in the outer circle, and then partner them (one inner circle member with one outer circle member). Inner circle members participate in the discussion, while the outer circle members observe based on their "observation form." Appoint one student to facilitate the discussion and have them begin the discussion with a partici-pant question or one that you have generated. At this point, the seminar begins. Any student can respond with their thoughts or with another question of their own.

Outer circle members follow the discussion carefully and look for the following attributes from the peer they observe:

	#of Times				
Offers a comment which demonstrated thought and ability to analyze					
Invited someone to speak					
Paraphrased what someone said					
Asked an interpretive question					
Referred to/cited the text/ learning material to support, defend, oppose an idea					
Identified a connection (personal, curriculum, other) with the text/ material					
Interrupted, used slang or rude language, made untimely commentary, etc.					

Outer circle members use this tally sheet to discuss key attributes and areas for improvement with their partner once the conversa-tion has concluded. After reflecting, have the outer circle and inner circle swap positions, and complete the Socratic Seminar again.

As a student-centered practitioner, I strongly recommend not interfering.

Yes, they may struggle, yes, they may interrupt each other, and yes, the conversation might get sidetracked or heated, but it's important that *they* self-correct. This will help them learn to resolve conflict on their own. Reflect and debrief with the whole class following the discussion and co-develop an anchor chart for expected behavior together. Your student facilitator can use this anchor chart to keep participants on track.

Here are five fabulous Socratic Seminar Topics if you want to model with the class before moving into your own content:

♦ The ethics of AI
♦ Climate Change and Responsibility
♦ Social Media and Personal Identity
♦ Impact of Technology on Mental Well-Being
♦ Ethics of Genetic Engineering

How might Socratic Seminars foster student-led discussion in your own context? What might it do for student engagement with your content and learning objectives?

Real World Forums, Round Table Discussions and Student Panels (MUN + GIN Conference)

"It is now time for a formal caucus to discuss sustainable solutions for the future. Would any delegate like to speak?"

Delegates from 13 countries raise their placards high in the air. The oldest member is only 16 years of age. For the next 15 minutes, student delegates representing more than 15 countries will discuss the actions their respective countries are taking to lower their carbon footprint and discuss ways to move the whole world in a positive direction at mitigating climate change. The result will be a formal proposal signed by all member nations.

Welcome to The Model United Nations Forum: An opportunity for students to act as real ambassadors to the UN.

This particular forum is one being run inside a courageous, learner-centered international school in Guatemala called Colegio Decroly Americano. The entire Year 9 came together during the last unit of the school year to help students participate and prepare. In Language Arts, they learned speaking skills and how to write a persuasive essay outlining their ideas; in biology, the interconnectedness of ecosystems; in history, the formation of the UN; in integrated math, data analysis and use of statistics; in Spanish, how to deliver a speech; art and music, performance in New York/Broadway. All subjects weaved together naturally to help students prepare for the MUN forum they would take part in to build sustainable solutions for the future.

How might you use a similar forum to facilitate student-led discussion in your class?

You don't have to include an entire grade level. You can unify a few classes around a single topic or big question. There are heaps of information on the internet around how to run Model United Nations Forums that include study guides; assessment criteria; speaking notes; and background information. And while many Model United Nations Clubs are delivered as an elective, what if we included these forums as part of our core classes?

They provide an authentic opportunity to bring core skills of public speaking, understanding varying perspectives, reaching consensus, compromise, listening respectfully to others, and paraphrasing to life.

If students unpacking global topics feels overwhelming, you can start with mini-debates on more lighthearted topics—like which fruit to include in the cafeteria's fruit salad bar? Each student can advocate for their favorite fruit. Rob Gold, MUN Coordinator at the International School of Manila, says these kinds of low-stakes debates make larger forums feel "more accessible for kids, as they don't have to do a lot of research. You can build in the language and structures of MUN-style debate and work them in really slowly and easily into what they will encounter in an MUN conference."

MUN is also an incredible mentorship opportunity for older peers. Older peers with more experience can mentor younger peers on the procedures and structures of the forum, including formal and informal caucus, speech writing, speaking in the third person, arguments and counter-arguments, and formal language.

How as a student-centered practitioner might you provide a space for these kinds of opportunities?

If you are interested in connecting to existing MUN conferences, you can find a comprehensive list using this database: https://bestdelegate.com/model-un-conferences-database/

Walk the Line and Four Corners

Ultimately if we are hoping to amplify student voice and collegial discussion in our classrooms, we are going to have to build in low risk structures that help them feel comfortable in using it. I had the pleasure of sitting in on a wonderful activity at The R.E.A.L. School Budapest that did just that:

> "Agree or Disagree: Utopian Societies need firm, authoritarian leadership." The facilitator prompted from her cross-legged position on the floor.

Students all moved to different points on an invisible line inside the large, open, mini- theater space. Those who strongly agreed stood on the far left while those who strongly disagreed stood on the far right. Most students were in the middle.

She then asked them to quickly pair/share with those next to them around why they agreed or disagreed with the statement and quickly formulate arguments. After time elapsed, she had them disseminate their ideas to the larger group. One boy raised his voice: "Societies that have weak leadership crumble quickly!" The facilitator asked him to share some examples. After naming a few historical examples, peers had the opportunity to probe his thinking and offer counter-arguments. At the same time, if they were persuasive to change their viewpoint, they also had the opportunity to move to a new point on the invisible line.

This was an entirely *student-run* discussion, with the learner-centered facilitator merely providing some starting points for discussion.

What debatable questions exist in your curriculum? How might you use this activity to help students gain confidence in sharing their opinion and listening to the viewpoint of others?

I watched one teacher engage students in a similar discussion activity around social justice, except this time, the line represented invisible privilege. After reading statements, students would take a step down the line if it applied to them. That is: "My parents both have college degrees." "I am a first language English speaker." By the time statements were finished, they were able to identify their respective starting point in the "privilege race."

Roundtable Discussions and Town Halls with Numerous Stakeholders

Once your students are comfortable with voicing their opinions, conducting discussions, and building consensus with peers, why not extend this to include stakeholders across the school and community? This is what Hong Kong University is providing students in its Generative AI Taskforce. Students review policies and procedures put forth by HKU around AI use during town hall meetings, and voice concerns, provide feedback, and offer their own solutions.

Alfie Chung, (mentioned earlier in the Chapter on Reflection) organized Town Hall Meetings for student stakeholders to share their input around the refurbishing and re-imagining of aban-doned buildings near their school. Their input, in addition to input from adult stakeholders across several relevant sectors, was given to an advisory board to help chart a pathway forward.

What if students also sat on that advisory board?

Barbara Anna Zielonka, a global educator and edtech spe-cialist is working with schools to do just that.

Through a strategic process of first raising awareness and interest and forming student interest groups; to developing a proposal and recruiting members, she discusses how students can drive the actual creation of these advisory boards to steer direction policy.

Some schools are already there! Students sit on the Advisory Board and represent various committees to help the school set strategic initiatives and develop relevant policy. South Island School in Hong Kong has student committees ranging from inclu-sion to sustainability. OneStone Academy in Idaho has a student advisory board that steers the admissions process and advises on teacher recruitment. At Templestowe College, more affection-ately known as "Take Control College," students are involved in nearly all decision making; they select 100 percent of their course load, have student-run electives, a student-run board, and create individualized learning plans that they co-wrote.

Peter Hutton, their past director and "Future Schools" founder says that it's all due to their "Yes Is Our Default Policy." "Any young person who wanted to change their experience of school in any way, the answer had to be yes."

This policy led to a variety of student electives and initiatives, including an automotive class to repair an abandoned car, and an actual zoo. Yes, students got a license to take care of animals ranging from guinea pigs to koala bears.

What might happen if you start saying "yes" more to your students? Providing them a space and forum to voice their opinions, and honoring what they have to share.

This doesn't have to be full-blown student-run school electives. It could be reconfiguring the timetable, choosing what topics they want to explore, where they choose to sit, or what resources help guide their learning. A lot of times, it's even simpler changes. Imagine my shock when during a democratic circle, students proposed a weekly digital packet to outline assignments, due dates, and linked resources. That was very doable!

After providing students a space to share opinions and put forth initiatives, how might you involve them in implementation? The student who proposed the weekly packets became my biggest asset in helping curate and organize the resources in a Google Slidedeck. The students who put forth the initiative to create a warmer learning environment were the same ones who purchased the rugs, lava lamps, and plug-in scents for various corners of the classroom.

Once we have empowered students to amplify their voice during student-led discussions, we will be ready to include them in our next shift, assessing and evaluating their learning.

Shift #9: Discussion and Decision-Making

Teacher-led < --- >Student-led, Socratic and Facilitated

	1	2	3	4	Now	Next
	Seedling (Sower)	Budding (Builder)	Blossoming (Beacon)	Flourishing (Facilitator)		
Discussion	Few to no learning experiences or open-ended discussions to support learning experiences. If there are, it's usually teacher-led from the front of the classroom.	Some discussions to support student inquiry and growth in learning experiences, but mostly teacher-led without clear scaffolding, protocols or processes to guide them. Some peer to peer teaching/learning.	Several discussions and resources support inquiry and growth in learning experiences w/ some student input and scaffolding, protocols or processes to guide them. Peer to peer teaching and learning taking place.	Socratic discussions, forums, and resources allow students to progressively dive deeper, teach each other and develop new insights within learning experiences. Teacher helps set up routines for these discussions initially but takes a "backseat" role, facilitating from behind the scenes. Lots of P2P teaching/learning.		

Reflective Questions

1. What scares you about inviting more student voices into the learning process? What are your hopes?
2. What opportunities do you currently provide for student to student discussion and decision making?
3. What ideas from this chapter do you think are most transferable within your context?

TEACHER-LED DISCUSSION

TEACHER MAKES ALL DECISIONS

TEACHER TALK > **STUDENT TALK**

SHA

TEXTBOOK OR TEACHER-GENERATED QUESTIONS

AND S

TEACHER-LED, DIDACTIC DISCUSSION

FEW INVISIBLE PLACES OF INPUT

NO ANCHOR RESOURCES

DISCUSSION DOMINATED BY ONE VOICE

IMAGE 9.2 Shift 9 Student-Led Discussion Infographic

STUDENT LED/ TEACHER FACILITATED

WNERSHIP

MULTIPLE ANCHOR RESOURCES (TEXT, VIDEO, EXPERIENCE, ETC)

TIC DISCUSSION

STUDENT GENERATED CO-CRAFTED OPEN QUESTIONS

TEACHER TALK < STUDENT TALK

**OTOCOLS AND
RMS ENSURE
LTIPLE PERSPECTIVES/
ICES ARE HEARD**

SUGGESTION BOX

VISIBLE PLACES FOR STUDENT INPUT

@kwagssd3

TRANSFORM
EDUCATIONAL CONSULTING

Part IV

Evaluating and Exhibiting Learning

10

Shift #10: From Progress Evaluated by the Teacher to Progress Fed Forward and Critiqued by Students, Peers, and Experts

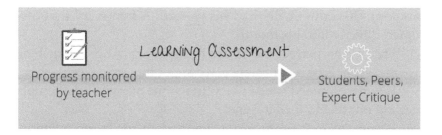

IMAGE 10.1 Shift 10 Collective and Shared Assessment

What can I give up that would make space for students to actually just focus on the quality of the work, rather than jumping through the external hoops for somebody else? For me, it was removing grades.

—Gary Heidt, English Teacher and Founder of
Nova Lab

DOI: 10.4324/9781003398226-15

Fritz is one of the most famous dogs on the internet.

There's a good chance you might have stumbled upon him when looking up "adorable dog" videos. You may have also found him when typing in "persistence."

I found him because I was searching for a novel way to introduce effective methods of assessment. Boring, I know. But when I was tipped off to Fritz by another learner-centered practitioner, I realized right away that he was the perfect opener.

In the three- minute video, Fritz sits patiently, awaiting a treat from his owner. As the owner tosses the treat high in the air, Fritz rises up on his hind legs and leaps into the air to catch it. The problem is, most of the time, the food doesn't land in his mouth. Most of the time it ricochets off his face and falls straight to the ground. Sometimes it misses his mouth entirely. In one attempt, a doughnut hits him square in the chest. In another attempt, he turns his head too early and a taco opens up on his left ear. In an even more awkward attempt, the backside of the pizza cheesifies his head.

But Fritz was determined. He used feedback from each attempt to alter his approach on the next. When the snack came, he remained glued to the ground; kept his eyes focused; and opened his mouth only after identifying the trajectory of the food. On attempt #10, Fritz finally had his reward: A french fry that caromed directly into his mouth.

Fritz is the perfect metaphor for learning. And as much as we marvel at Fritz's persistence, we aren't that much unlike him.

When we learned to ride a bicycle, we had many failed attempts getting our feet to turn in sync.

When we learned to swim, we had many failed attempts keeping our heads and legs above water.

When we learned to cook food, we had many failed attempts in getting the right mixture of ingredients.

We learn from regular feedback on failed attempts.

Imagine if we were evaluated on our ability to ride a bike after only our first attempt.

Or judged on the quality of our pasta after cooking it for the very first time.

Too often this is the way we assess learning in school. Students are doomed to fail from the start. In a race against time and curricular coverage, we offer few opportunities for students to reflect, reattempt, and receive feedback. We award arbitrary point values and letter grades on first and second attempts of learning, rather than specific feedback around student strengths and how they can improve. We value measurement over mastery.

But what happens when we have the courage to ask the same question Gary Heidt, founder of the Nova Lab, asked in re-considering how he assesses learning:

> What can I give up that would make space for students to actually just focus on the quality of the work, rather than jumping through the external hoops for somebody else?
>
> —Gary Heidt, English Teacher and
> Founder of Nova Lab

I know what you might be thinking. How are we supposed to offer personalized feedback when some of us have 25–30 students per class? Multiplied by the four to five preps we teach, that's over 100 students on any given day. We don't have the luxury of a 1:1 teacher to pupil ratio like Fritz and his owner.

I totally get that. Personalized assessment becomes infinitely more challenging the more students we are responsible for teaching. But what if we weren't the only ones responsible for assessment in our classrooms? What if we made assessment a collectively owned process managed by self, peers, and experts? What if we developed a culture where students were able to offer customized, specific feedback on their peers' work? Provided students with the tools to assess their own learning and demonstrate competence and mastery of relevant skills?

With a little re-imagining and restructuring of our assessment methods, we can shift from…

Teacher-assessed learning - - - - - - - - - - - - - - - > Students, peers, teacher, and expert feedback/critique

Competency/Mastery-Based Reporting

Before moving into micro-tips, strategies, and insights for how to make assessment an effective and collectively owned process in our individual classrooms, I think it's imperative to give an overview of the macro-shifts happening in schools. Several schools are shifting away from a points-based, letter grade/GPA method of reporting to a competency or mastery-based system of assessing and reporting. The impetus is to offer a clearer picture around what students are able to do. Competencies include traits like "collaborate effectively," "think critically," "communicate competently," and "create divergently." Each competency includes a breakdown of the skills required to meet it, and individual statements of what those skills look like in action. For example, "communicate competently" might include a sub-skill of "spoken and visual communication" and a supporting statement of "I can tailor my presentations to specific and relevant audiences." Students are responsible for gathering artifacts of each competency through various projects, assignments, and work they complete in and out of school.

This competency report, or Mastery Based Transcript, is supplementing, and in some cases replacing the traditional transcript in many high schools around the world. It's easy to see why. A Mastery Transcript provides a far better insight into the individual talents, strengths, skills, abilities and interests of each student than a traditional GPA. With this level of articulation, universities can more accurately assess whether or not a student will be a good fit for their school, and students can have a better starting point for the conversation. And while it's still in its infancy, the Mastery Transcript Consortium already has 372 member schools.

But it's not just the Mastery Transcript Consortium Schools that are bidding farewell to traditional letter grades and transcripts.

Vocational, Career Technical Education (CTE), and other innovative programs around the world have developed their own unique competencies to fit their settings. For example, KTEC, an interdisciplinary, technical charter school in Kenosha, Wisconsin, assesses student learning against its ten unique competencies including

Global Citizenship, Quantitative Reasoning, Meaningful Research, and Solutions Focused. Students earn competency "badges" after fulfilling all of the skills required in each competency. Within "quantitative reasoning," these include skills like "using systematic methods to identify patterns" and "creating models to represent mathematical information." Verso International School, the interdisciplinary citizenship minded school mentioned several times in previous chapters, has developed its unique model that assesses student learning against co-constructed proficiencies. These proficiencies include Communication, Ventures, Humanism, Inquiry, Thinking, and Self. The Ventures proficiency includes individual skills like advocacy, networking, mentoring, and enterprise. Students progress through each proficiency level, from novice to mentor, through performance on authentic formative and summative assessments within the context of longer learning experiences.

The International Baccalaureate, the largest governing body of international schools in the world, assesses student proficiency in each subject against broader criteria as well. Rather than award students a grade in geometry or algebra, math classrooms report out individually on the criterion of "knowing and understanding," "investigating patterns," "communicating," and "applying mathematics in real life concepts." Assessing learning in this way helps students connect subject-specific content to broader concepts, and interdisciplinary ways of thinking.

Even the Common Core Curriculum in the United States has shifted away from assessing a breadth of knowledge and into assessing larger transferable competencies like "Presentation of Ideas" and "Comprehension and Collaboration."

All of this is excellent news for us as student-centered practitioners. It shifts assessment away from the minutiae of content standards and into broader, more transferable skills. It also frees us from the burden of having to assess every single piece of student work and, instead, allows us to make assessment an ongoing, reflective, collective process toward broader competencies.

So how do we achieve this in our student-centered environments? Below are multiple ideas from student-centered classrooms just like yours.

Self-Assessment

A group of elementary students stand shoulder to shoulder, shading their eyes from the bright spring sun outside the YWIS campus in Rizhao, China. Their eyes focus on their beloved facilitator, Mrs. Lua, dressed in a gigantic blue-billed cap, T-shirt, and jeans. She picks up a handful of dirt and describes the quality of the soil, referencing its texture and composition. She asks students to note their observations. They have a conversation around things they see like color and structure, as well as unseen characteristics of nutrient content, organic matter, and moisture. And while they don't have the testing equipment to measure these things now, she explains that they will be testing these things in a few days' time.

Soil testing is only the start of a longer unit of study that will ask students to transform the barren field outside of their classroom into a beautiful growing space. She guides her eager six-to-ten-year-olds back into the classroom. Rather than drop a project packet onto their desk, she invites them to co-create expectations with her. "What do you think we will need to know and learn to take on this project?"

Students devise questions around seasons, soil condition, types of plants, growing conditions, weather patterns, and how to journal observations. Lua writes each of these topics onto the board and begins to categorize into competencies based on similarities. One category is "Recognizing Patterns." Whether they are aware of it or not, students are co-creating the criteria for how they will be assessed, written in a language they understand. After all, many of them are second language learners.

Lua's co-created rubric is one of the most valuable tools for self- assessment. Assessment criteria is explicit, easy to understand, and aligns with the expectations of the deeper learning experience. Lua would go on to set up regular times throughout the learning for students to self-assess against their co-created expectations. As students conducted research, completed observation journals, developed soil studies, chose what to plant, built planter beds, and developed presentations for their peers, Lua constantly directed their attention back to the co-created rubric to assess their progress. The rubric was double-sided so Lua could assess according to her own observations and 1:1 conferencing. It provided a springboard for learners to discuss their current strengths and establish goals for successive check-ins.

In addition to rubrics, Lua worked with learners to develop checklists for the various products they would develop. They co-created these checklists based on models from the real world. Students looked at field notes from real scientists, garden designs from real horticulturists, and presentations from real graphic designers. These helped them identify what to include in their own field studies, journals, proposed design, and pitch for their peers.

Empowering students to self-assess freed time and space for Lua to act as a learning facilitator. She could check-in with more learners, meet with students in small groups, and individualize tasks.

It can do the same for us.

How might you empower students to self-assess in your own context? It doesn't have to be a four-week-long learning experience. It could be a short two-to-three-lesson science experiment, open-ended math problem, writing piece, short film, unit of study, design challenge, or travel diary. Bonnie Nieves, a learner-centered science teacher, works with her learners to co-create proficiency rubrics around her science standards. To effectively scaffold the process, she uses six simple steps:

1. First, she writes her own proficiency five-scale rubric and discusses with learners. In this case it was around homeostasis

2. Next, periodically through the unit, she draws attention to the language in the scale and aligns it to the goals, learning opportunities, and knowledge demonstration tasks students undertake

3. Students self-assess at various points and brainstorm ways to demonstrate understanding of each concept (i.e., What problems might a person be able to solve with knowledge of homeostasis? What advanced inferences

and authentic connections of homeostasis can you make? What activities have you completed that demonstrate a "negative feedback" loop?)

4. When students are familiar with the format, they build the scale together. Bonnie provides students with a standard, and after explaining her goals, works with students to discuss what a person with proficiency in that standard should be able to do

5. As they move through the learning process, together, they populate the rest of the scale to determine what is most essential

6. Eventually, once students are familiar with the process of rubric co-creation, they can develop their own, in addition to personalizing their own "exceeding expectations" or "exceeding proficiency" box with their own independent deeper investigation or authentic project

Through inviting students into the process of assessment, Bonnie has a room full of learners thinking more deeply about her content. The culture around assessment has changed from "testing what students know," to "show me what you can do."[1]

Next time when introducing a unit, concept, topic, project, or extended activity, I wonder what might happen if after hooking learners, you shared this …

Criteria	Emerging	Approaching	Meeting	Exceeding
	I can demonstrate evidence of initial and/or inconsistent understanding of concepts, skills, and/or processes within the standard	I can demonstrate with some consistency, evidence of partial understanding of concepts, skills, and/or processes within the standard.	I can demonstrate evidence of thorough and consistent understanding of concepts, skills, and/or processes within the standard	I can demonstrate the ability to transfer concepts, skills, and/or processes beyond the standard
Standard A				
Standard B				

… and designed it together. More around teacher assessment later.

Peer Feedback and Critique

In student-centered environments, everyone is a teacher. We probably have students in our math classes who are two grade levels ahead; students in our technology classes who know advanced programming languages; learners in our language classes that have written their own books. It's our job to create the kind of environment that empowers these learners to support and share their learning with their peers.

This kind of learning happens in Montessori classrooms on a daily basis.

I still remember walking into my first Montessori Classroom five years ago. Small groups of students huddled around a peer teacher, equipped with a folding whiteboard easel, finger pointer, and a set of markers. One brown-haired girl with thick glasses taught their peers how to solve for unknown variables. On the other side of the room, a young, short-haired boy taught peers how to write opening hooks for their writing pieces. In another corner, a girl with thick curls taught peers new vocabulary words. The Montessori Teacher had her own mini-lesson. She was helping students understand the characteristics of different biomes.

Walk in on a different day, and you wouldn't be surprised to find new student teachers supporting their peers in learning new concepts. This peer teaching culture extended beyond just peer-to-peer learning; it also extended into peer assessment, feedback, and critique. It wasn't unusual to find two students conferencing over a peer's writing piece or huddled around a screen with a presentation that a student was looking for feedback on.

Empowering students to be peer teachers and evaluators takes time, but with the right language, frames, tools, and protocols, we, too, can instill this kind of peer assessment and feedback culture within our own classrooms.

"'Austin's Butterfly" is one of my favorite starting points. This short clip depicts a critique session led by the infamous learner-centered practitioner Ron Berger (also mentioned in the Reflection Chapter). Ron helped to support a small-group peer-critique session in an Idaho first grade in which a student, Austin, improves his scientific drawing of a swallow-tailed butterfly. In this video, he shares with students in another school the drafts that Austin created and encourages them to imagine what kinds of critique he received in order to improve. Austin had illustrated the butterfly as part of a larger set of note cards his class was creating to raise funds to support butterfly habitats in Idaho. As Ron takes students through each of Austin's drafts, he asks students to critique the work with clear parameters. "Our first critique is going to be just the shape of the wings. After the shape is right, we are going to provide advice on the patterns of the wings." One student points out that the wings need to be pointier, while another observes that the wings need to extend farther on the page. In the next draft, the wings need to face "in the right direction." On a successive draft, Austin's wings need "inside notches." On the next, "a more clear angle." By the time Ron puts up the last draft, Austin's butterfly drawing is almost an exact replica of the scientific drawing he was trying to emulate.

The class is amazed, Austin is pleased, and Ron's skillful facilitation has supported the process.

What takeaways around effective peer feedback might you pull from the video? You might notice that students use precise language, carefully consider what they say, or deliver each piece of critique with compassion. Ron has only three simple rules: Be kind, helpful, and specific.

After watching and reflecting on the video clip, you could have students practice implementing these three rules by critiquing a new film, video game, restaurant, building design, YouTube ad, or ride at an amusement park. Ask for them to use precise and specific language to share its strengths and potential areas for improvement. Frame the critique like Ron did by having students look for specific elements. "What can we say about the ad's message? How effective was it?" Ask students for "warm" and "cool" feedback using the feedback sentence starters below:

Warm Feedback	Cool Feedback
I'm struck by …	I wonder …
I like the way …	I'm confused by …
A strength of _____ is _____ …	I want to know more about …
My favorite part was …	Might you consider …
The work displays …	Can you clarify …

Critiquing work from outside the classroom will help you build the structures and language for how to critique within the classroom. According to Ron

> It's not hard for students to get great at this because they spend all their free time critiquing. They critique clothes. They critique music. They critique pop culture. They critique each other's hairstyles, like they critique endlessly in their life. All we're doing is harnessing that energy of critique and putting it in a safe, useful way in class.

In my opinion, the safest, most useful way to transition from outside critique to classroom peer critique is through the use of gallery walks. A gallery walk is a guided process that allows peers to move around the room to observe and leave feedback on their peers' work in a private setting. This could be printed pieces of work like a drawing, illustration, diagram, infographic, or short piece of writing, or a digital piece of work like an animation, video game, short video, CAD rendering, and so forth. Here's how to run it:

- ◆ Students prepare their own work sample and put it on display for peers.
- ◆ Next, as individuals, students rotate to a free piece of work to offer feedback.
- ◆ Armed with a pen and Post-Its, after carefully observing, they write two "glows" (strengths of the work) and one "grow" (area for improvement) onto their Post-It notes.

Some teachers use the terminology "two stars and a wish" or "warm" and "cool" feedback.

◆ They place the Post-Its next to the work sample and move onto another peer's work.

◆ After a set amount of time (20 minutes is generally ideal), have learners return to their own piece of work to review the feedback. I generally ask learners to pick at least two pieces of feedback they received that will be most useful for them in successive drafts. Sometimes I ask a few volunteers to share this publicly so we can honor the feedback provider and affirm our norms around high-quality feedback.

Gallery walks can be equally, if not more, effective in a digital landscape. Zach Post, the principal of American International School Hong Kong, introduced me to a highly effective method called Window Shopping. Participants put up their work for review on separate Google Slides for peers to "window shop" and leave feedback. Zach and I have both used this strategy for reviewing teacher project plans but you might use it for students to provide feedback on peers' artistic concepts, cover designs, ideas, logos, and the like. Another common tool that works well for digital gallery walks and peer feedback is Padlet. You can organize a shared padlet into columns around different kinds of work or sub-topics and have students post their work for review. They can even indicate in the summary section a specific part of their work they would like feedback on.

How might gallery walks build a culture around high-quality critique in your classroom?

You might time them around major milestones for deep, whole-class learning experiences; or at more infrequent intervals with individual student project work or assignments.

The more guided gallery walks you conduct, the more likely students will be to seek out peer feedback on their own.

Formal Peer Assessment

Peers can even support us in formal assessment of learning. Equipped with the self-assessment rubrics developed using strategy #1, peers can offer an additional lens on their peers' work and targeted learning objectives. This strategy is especially useful with end of unit, summative tasks. Students can provide their evidence of work to peers, and using clear, co-created objectives and criteria for evaluation, the peers can provide an evaluation that can easily supplement yours. If there is a discrepancy between yours and the students' self evaluation, you can use their peer's evaluation to provide clarification. This happens in the real world all the time with 360 performance reviews. Employees receive evaluations from a number of peers to help them identify their major strengths and areas for improvement. I recently underwent a process similar to 360 reviews when evaluating teachers' planned learning experiences. Equipped with a clear rubric and a website with numerous artifacts around the learning submitted by the teacher team, I was easily able to provide a rating. The head coordinator will use this rating along with two other peer reviewers to award a final mark.

Google Forms are also useful for conducting anonymous peer-to-peer evaluations, and I find they work especially well with evaluating team members. Peers can assess their peers against a number of criteria including "willingness to compromise," "timeliness," "follow through on deadlines," and other relevant criteria. I have included a sample rubric around team collaboration for easy reference below.

Moving to Public, Group Critique

Are you an *American Idol* fan? If you aren't familiar with the show, it's essentially a singing contest where contestants perform original or cover songs in an attempt to move on to successive rounds. The only thing standing in their way? Three judges. And although judges have changed from season to season, most people remember the originals. Paula Abdul was the kindhearted softie who had nothing but glowing reviews for every performer. Randy Jackson was the judge who couldn't get through a sentence of feedback without uttering "yo dawg." And Simon Cowell was the judge who made some contestants wince in fear before he even opened his mouth (even though as he says, he was "just being honest").

Communication and Collaboration

(Modified from open-source PBL 21st Century Skills Rubrics -www.pblworks.org

Individual Performance	Emerging	Approaching	Target
Taking Responsibility for Myself	Collaboration		
	❏ I struggle with being prepared, informed, and ready to work with my team ❏ I can start tasks but have difficulty completing them ❏ I struggle to complete tasks in a timely manner ❏ I generally need support from a team leader or teacher to get started on tasks	❏ I am usually prepared, informed, and ready to work with my team ❏ I do some project tasks, but I often need to be reminded regarding next steps ❏ I complete most tasks on time	❏ I am prepared and ready to work; a well read and informed on the proj topic and cite evidence to probe a reflect on ideas with my team (cc 6-12.SL.1a) ❏ I take initiative for completing tasks and do not have to be reminded ❏ I complete tasks on time and to completion
	Communication		
	❏ It is difficult for me to use technology and other communication tools as agreed upon by my team in order to communicate and manage project tasks ❏ I struggle with using feedback from others to improve work	❏ I use technology and other communication tools as agreed upon by the team to communicate and manage project tasks, but not consistently ❏ I sometimes use feedback from others to improve project work	❏ I consistently use technology and other communication tools as agre upon by my team to communicate and manage project tasks ❏ I use feedback from others to improve my work within a project
Helping my Team	Collaboration		
	❏ I have difficulty helping my team solve problems; sometimes I may cause problems ❏ I struggle with offering help to others if they need it	❏ I cooperate with my team but may not actively help it solve problems ❏ I sometimes offer to help others to complete work if needed	❏ I actively help my team solve problems and manage conflicts ❏ I offer to help others complete the work if needed
	Communication		
	❏ I provide input but struggle with asking probing questions, expressing ideas, or elaborating in response to questions in discussions ❏ I give feedback but find it difficult to give kind, helpful and specific feedback to others	❏ I sometimes expresses ideas clearly, ask probing questions, and elaborate in response to questions in discussions ❏ I give kind, helpful and specific feedback to others, but it may not always be useful	❏ I make discussions effective by clearly expressing ideas, asking probing questions, making sure everyone is heard, responding thoughtfully to new information an perspectives (CC 6-12.SL.1c) ❏ I give kind, helpful and specific feedback (specific, feasible, supportive) to team members so th can improve their work
Respecting Others	Collaboration		
	❏ I struggle being polite or kind to my teammates (I may interrupt, ignore ideas, or hurt feelings) ❏ I have difficulty acknowledging or respecting other perspectives	❏ I am usually polite and kind to my teammates ❏ I usually acknowledge and respect other perspectives and disagree diplomatically	❏ I am polite and kind to my teamm ❏ I acknowledge and respect other perspectives; I disagree diplomatically

IMAGE 10.2 Co-created Assessment Rubric

The truth is, like *American Idol* contestants, our learners prefer how they receive feedback. Some need a tender Paula; others need a personable Randy; and some need a straight shooter like Simon. Before conducting public critique, I always like to ask learners how they would like their feedback. "Do you want Paula, Randy, or Simon?" It's also a useful question for peers to pose. It helps honor the feelings, sensitivities, and preferences of the student presenter.

As a student-centered practitioner, you probably have already discovered that public critique requires the most skillful facilitation. Many of our students are terrified of being shamed when standing in front of their peers. Prior to critiquing student work publicly, I would suggest modeling public critique using a formal protocol first. And while there are a plethora of critique protocols available for free from the National Reform Faculty (at https://nsrfharmony.org/protocols/), here is my favorite that you can easily adapt for your context:

1. **Present Work/Plan/Proposal for Critique**: Presenter shares piece of work/plan/proposal and asks if there is any specific area where they would like to receive feedback.
2. **Clarifying Questions**: Peer critiquers ask clarifying questions of the presenter around the work. (that is, Can you remind me of the intended audience for your work? Did you make changes to earlier drafts?)
3. **Probing Questions**: Probing questions present an opportunity for students to ask deeper questions into student thinking around the work. (What do you hope this work achieves? Is there a part of this work you are most proud of? Can you take me through your process of creation?)
4. **Group Discussion**: At this time, the presenter turns their back to the group. This is to allow the group to have an open discussion. The group discusses the strengths and areas for potential improvement. Use the stems "I appreciate," "I wonder," "I wish." The presenter takes notes.
5. **Reflection**: The presenter is invited back to the group to share what they heard and changes they are considering to enhance their work.

I cannot overstress the importance of modeling this process first with a piece of your own work. Modeling how to receive feedback and reflect more deeply on your work will open the door for students to be more reflective of their own. Model with them how to say "thank you" in response to each piece of feedback, no matter how harsh; model how to respond concisely to clarifying questions; and model responding thoughtfully to probing questions.

"Hard on the content, soft on the people." This was our motto for providing feedback at High Tech High, and ensured we focused our feedback on the work itself, not the person.

Expert Feedback, Critique, and Assessment

As student-centered practitioners, we already know we aren't the only experts in the room. And while we already discussed the expertise our students can provide peers in evaluation and feedback, how about real-world experts outside of the classroom? What happens to student work when real architects are evaluating and offering feedback on their blueprints for an upgraded playground? Real scientists on their water studies? Real authors on their short stories? Real mathematicians on their method of data collection?

This is how Ron Berger helps students improve their work. Every Friday, he would bring in professionals to look at student work and offer kind, helpful, and specific feedback. Here's Ron around his student's response to visit from local architects to offer feedback on student's Victorian Playhouse:

> It gave them such motivation to have their scale drawings correct, to have their mathematics correct, to have everything drawn to code, to understand what building codes were, and then the architects would always take certain pieces of work that they noticed and put it on the board. They would say, let's see what's working in this piece. Why were you thinking this? Why were you thinking that?

Matt Neylon, Learner Centered Practitioner and Art Director of Mount Vernon High School, uses outside experts as adjudicators and mentors in many of his learning experiences as well. During one extended learning experience on creating startups, he had executives from Porsche evaluate the students' market research findings. They were blown away. He proudly recalls, "They said, 'This is better than the last market research study we did, which we paid six figures for.'"

You don't have to fly in expert executives from Porsche to have experts evaluate student work. Oftentimes expertise can come from the room next door. We had art teachers evaluate and offer feedback on our students' logo designs when they were developing their own small businesses. The facilities department offered feedback on students' 21st-century space design when designing more inclusive classrooms. Expertise can also come from our parents. I've seen physical education teachers invite parent nutritionists and wellness experts to offer feedback on student's well-being plans. I've seen a social studies teacher invite an archaeologist to help students conduct a proper archaeological dig.

How might you involve experts in helping critique and offer feedback for your student's work?

You might start with a parent letter before launching a new learning experience or unit of study. Share your goals and ask if anyone has expertise in a relevant area. You could reach out to friends. I had a friend who worked in a local city council office help me run a mock council meeting with students around drafting energy laws. You might reach out on social media through the relevant community pages. I've seen teachers elicit expertise from experts on opposite ends of the globe through a single post that shared what they were looking for. You might reach out via email or telephone.

But the greatest chance for success in eliciting expertise will come from students reaching out themselves. It's easy to turn down a teacher, but infinitely harder to turn down an idealistic eight-year-old. Have a discussion with students around the learning experience and brainstorm together what professionals in the real world might be able to assist. Perhaps they might even know someone.

Back at school these experts can sit on adjudication panels, serve as individual project mentors, share details around the day-to-day nature of their work, deliver a lecture, unpack professional processes, and even offer to lend equipment. Best of all, they will add a layer of authenticity and rigor to student work.

Teacher Assessment and Feedback in Student-Centered Environments

Despite how involved peers and experts are in assessing student learning, students are still going to want to hear from us. And in most cases, we are obligated to provide a final mark. But most of us have liberty in how we get there. First, shift assessment away from the accumulation of points and disconnected assignments. Instead, connect learning to larger learning goals/objectives and assess students against their progress toward them. We also need to offer students multiple opportunities to demonstrate competency. As student-centered practitioners, we cannot expect learners to understand a concept right away.

When our Year 7 students developed proposals for sustainable growing systems, it was impossible to evaluate them after one week. Instead, we offered feedback on their initial ideas; methods for conducting research; and around how they analyzed collected data. This feedback was guided by the learning objectives we established at the onset. As students progressed through their learning, feedback transformed into more formal evaluations. For example, when students submitted their formal proposals around their method of food production, they were assessed against the organization of information, graphing of data, visualization of their food growing techniques, and use of argumentative reasoning. These were all explicit objectives co-articulated with students and put into age-appropriate language that could be easily assessed in their work products.

Other informal 1:1 conversations, observations, exit tickets, activities, or small group presentations. Just like careful ethnographers, we should have a multitude of data points for overall evaluation of student learning. Below is a sample teacher assessment plan for the Phoenix Project mentioned above, that asked students to develop Sustainable Future Societies.

Learning Targets/Competency and Strands	Socratic Seminars	Research	Proposal	Observations	Presentations	Food System Prototype	Inquiry Journal
Competent Communicator							
I can write in an organized, fluent, and informative style (writing)							
I can use argumentative reasoning and evidence to defend my method of food production and refute counter-arguments							
I can apply scientific ideas, principles, and evidence to support a claim							
I can use technology to publish and enhance writing and presentations							
Speaking							
I can participate in a range of collaborative discussions, express ideas, and build on others							
I can incorporate multimedia elements and visual displays to present information clearly							

Learning Targets/Competency and Strands	Socratic Seminars	Research	Proposal	Observations	Presentations	Food System Prototype	Inquiry Journal
I can use appropriate eye contact, body language, tone, and clear pronunciation to communicate ideas							
Investigating and Inquiring							
I can construct and use models to represent and analyze systems							
I can formulate, refine, and evaluate testable questions and define problems							
I can collect and analyze data using models to determine relationships between variables							
I can synthesize ideas, claims, details and evidence from multiple, diverse sources							
Confident Creator							
I can use ingenuity and imagination, going outside conventional boundaries when shaping ideas into a product							

Note how many opportunities we provided students to demonstrate competency. Also note the way competencies worked together seamlessly across traditional bounds in the products (top row) students developed. Note as well the specificity of each learning target.

How as a student-centered practitioner, might you use this more holistic approach to assessment to evaluate and offer feedback to your learners? How might you connect learning to deeper goals, rather than disconnected one-off lessons and activities?

With students, experts, and peers involved, I am confident you can make assessment a more inclusive process in your classroom.

Here's a chart that helps articulate each assessment shift:

Teacher-Centered Assessment	Student-Centered Assessment
Knowledge Based	Competency Based
Doesn't Diagnose Readiness and Prior Background	Diagnosis Readiness and Prior Background
Grade Based	Opportunities for ongoing feedback, reflection
Vague Criteria	Explicit criteria
Evaluation Based	Feedback, Growth Based
Single Evaluation Measure	Multiple Ways to Demonstrate Learning
Mostly High Stakes/Exam Based	Mostly Low Stakes
Teacher Created	Co-created
Inauthentic, School Based Contexts	Authentic, Real-World Contexts
Mostly Summative Measures	Mix of Formative and Summative Measures

Shift #10: Assessment of Learning

Teacher assessed < ———————————— >Student, peer, expert, teacher feedback and critique

	1	2	3	4	Now	Next
	Seedling (Sower)	Budding (Builder)	Blossoming (Beacon)	Flourishing (Facilitator)		
Task Completion	Teacher assesses all work within learning experiences.	Students have some input in how they are evaluated/assessed, but few opportunities to reflect on their growth, and usually in isolation. Teacher sets up only limited time to conference and set goals for future work.	Some structures set up for management/evaluation of work with peers, self and teacher. Teacher makes an attempt to co-design criteria and evaluation methods with students, but may be lacking examples of model work to guide the process. Relevant experts within the community are used only for evaluation, not as mentors to help support students in the process.	A relevant combination of students, peers and experts provides continual feedback on student work, both in process of completion, and in the product. Students co-develop methods of evaluation with teacher input. Experts also utilized as mentors/coaches.		

Reflective Questions

1. How might you involve learners in assessment and evaluation of their learning experiences?
2. How might you make feedback and critique a more regular, ongoing part of the learning journey?
3. How can you ensure learning in your classroom connects to larger goals?

TEACHER-LED ASSESSMENT

SINGLE HIGH STAKES ASSESMENT

ONE WHOLE CLASS PRESENTATION AT END

VAGUE ASSESMENT CRITERIA

STUDE

TEACHER AS EVALUATOR

GRADE BASED FEEDBACK

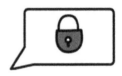

S
FEE

FEEDBACK IS HIDDEN

TEACHER MANAGES PROJECTS

NO NORMS FOR PEER FEEDBACK

@ kwagssd3

© 2020 Kyle Wagner and Rob Riordan

TRANSFORM
EDUCATIONAL CONSULTING

IMAGE 10.3 Shift 10 Teacher to Collective and Shared Assessment Infographic

STUDENT, PEER, EXPERT, CRITIQUE

MANAGE PROJECTS

NARRATIVE BASED FEEDBACK

REVIEW

**EER & EXPERT
K AND CRITIQUE**

**EAR, CO-CREATED
SESSMENT CRITERIA**

FEEDBACK IS PUBLIC, GUIDED BY NORMS

NORMS + PROTOCOLS
FOR FEEDBACK/CRITIQUE

SMALL SHARING SESSIONS THROUGHOUT

EVIDENCE OF GROWTH

Note

1 https://docs.google.com/document/d/17ArcoLj51eNSxuns
  oyJQpw1QuIBTQmq5I_Xkks8JVEk/edit?usp=sharing

Bibliography

Berger, Ron. "Austin's Butterfly: Models, Critique, and Descriptive Feedback." *YouTube*, 4 Oct. 2016, www.youtube.com/watch?v=E_6PskE3zfQ

"Building an 'ethic of Excellence' with Ron Berger." *Transformative Learning Experiences with Kyle Wagner*, transformschool.libsyn.com/building-an-ethic-of-excellence-with-ron-berger. Accessed 14 Oct. 2023.

11

Shift #11: From Teacher Audience to Authentic, Public Audience

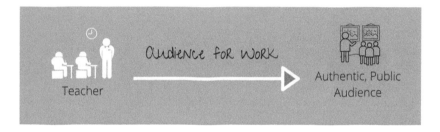

IMAGE 11.1 Shift 11 Building Authentic Audiences for Student Work

> One of the most important things is that the work has to go beyond your desk. The part that gets the kids is [having a real audience]. You mean I not only have to write a book, but I'm presenting it at my local bookshop? I'm publishing it on Kindle, and I get to sell it and make money? Oh yeah. That makes me wanna do that.
>
> —Alexa Lepp, Learner-Centered Practitioner

As a student-centered practitioner, how do you usually conclude units of study or extended learning experiences?

Most teacher-centered classrooms end with an exam: The perfect mechanism for the holder of all knowledge to assess students on everything they taught.

DOI: 10.4324/9781003398226-16

There is little to no room for student agency, voice, creativity, or students' own meaning making.

But what if learning didn't end in an exam, but a real showcase of learning for a community outside of the classroom?

That's how students at student-centered powerhouse the Creative School of Hong Kong conclude their learning journeys (pictured below).

IMAGE 11.2 Student-Led Public Exhibition

Students regularly curate exhibitions like these to showcase real-world product and work, and retell the learning journey that got them there.

And it's magical.

I listened to one biology student share his journey of developing an aquaponics system for the roof of his school; another humanities student shares her journey of developing a hand-carved pop-up book to retell community stories; and business students share their journey of partnering with craftsmen to revitalize local handicraft businesses.

It's amazing what students can create when the audience extends beyond the four walls of their classroom.

How about you? Where do your students exhibit their work?

We spoke a lot around creating authentic opportunities for students to develop work in previous chapters, but what about creating opportunities for students to share and showcase that work? This chapter centers around moving from a siloed, teacher-based audience for student work to a public, community based audience. We will explore ideas from real student-centered practitioners like yourself around how to find audiences, curate the work, and transform students into polished presenters.

To begin that journey, I want you to close your eyes and take an imaginary trip to your favorite museum. As you walk through the doors, what catches your eye? Which exhibits are most captivating? Imagine yourself traveling to the exhibit and carefully observing the way they have been constructed.

For me, the exhibit that comes to mind immediately is a "Journey through Time" at the Museum of Man. The room is circular. And that's intentional. Its design is intended to demonstrate the interconnectedness of our human ancestors- from *Australopithecus afarensis* to modern-day *Homo sapiens*. As you move through each stage of evolution, glass cases enclose bones, skulls, pottery, and artifacts they left behind. Video simulations demonstrate how they might have lived. An interactive map projected on the wall allows you to trace their journey with your fingers and probe deeper into how they inhabited each continent.

So what's museum curation have to do with our classrooms?

A lot more than we think.

Imagine if student work was curated in the same way it was in a museum: Iterations carefully laid out to demonstrate each step of the journey; artifacts of learning enclosed in glass cases; projectors to help engage the audience in deeper investigation. Students as docents—ready to share their process of curation.

At High Tech High, we held these schoolwide exhibitions of learning once a year. At Expeditionary Learning Schools, it was at the end of each learning expedition. In PYP (Primary Years Programme Schools) schools, it's at the end of Year 5. And in

MYP (Middle Years Programme) schools, student's exhibition of work follows the completion of their Personal Projects.

In these exhibitions, the whole community is invited.

But exhibiting work doesn't have to be so large-scale. You can exhibit to the classroom next door. I've witnessed exhibitions where older primary students authored and shared children's books with younger peers three doors down. Small scale TED Talk exhibitions where graduating seniors shared lessons learned for junior peers a floor below. Innovation Fairs, where an entire year level occupied the gymnasium for a day, to share their inventions with classmates.

Providing opportunities for these public exhibitions takes far more imagination than it does expert coordination.

First, it requires us to engage students in authentic work. As mentioned previously, we need to allow students to work like real anthropologists, scientists, and mathematicians. But there is another layer of authenticity that's often overlooked: The *audience* for that work. Remember Thomas Bivens and his "Thai Heroes" book writing project back in Chapter 5? He brought in more than just his students' parents to marvel at the books their children wrote; he also brought in the Thai heroes as well. Imagine seeing your story put in print for the very first time in your very own hardcover book.

In student-centered practitioner Zoe Randall's semester-long "Stories of Service" experience, her students curated a screening of war veterans' firsthand narratives of their experiences in combat. They invited the veterans to hear each story. There were hardly enough tissue boxes in the room to dry the eyes of World War II veterans who watched their stories visualized for the first time on the big screen by tenth graders! Secondary Student-Centered practitioner Kimberly Williams's drama students put on a Social Change Film Festival for the community to inspire action around important issues. In attendance were influential non-profits who could amplify that change.

Who might your students present their work to? How might you engage this audience at regular intervals throughout the learning process?

Here are a few ways to engage with audiences outside of the classroom. They can:

- ◆ Serve as adjudicators for student work
- ◆ Provide insights and expertise around what learning in the classroom looks like in the real world
- ◆ Frame the challenge students will address in their work
- ◆ Serve as mentors for students as they develop ideas, work samples, and products
- ◆ Carry students' work forward to a wider community and key stakeholders
- ◆ Provide community spaces for exhibition

Community Curation

Putting our students' work on public display is not easy. Oftentimes it's hard to let go.

During my first student exhibition of work at High Tech High, I curated most of it. I put my highfliers' work at the front of the room and moved the "weaker students" to the back. I provided each student a scripted template, strict parameters around how they organized their booths, and stood at the front of the classroom to welcome parents when they came through the doors.

It was essentially the "Kyle Wagner Show" with a supporting cast of characters. As a result, most of my students' work looked the same: A framed one-page written product, small accompanying artifact, and a uniform slide deck to share the process with parents. It was uninspiring.

One of my educational mentors/personal heroes challenged me to re-imagine exhibitions through student eyes. What did they want to share? What was meaningful to them? What would help them take more ownership of the exhibition?

I used these questions to guide the next exhibition of work: Ancient Egypt Living Museums. I told my Year 6 students I would be taking a step back during the exhibition, and that they would be curating it entirely on their own. It was their job to re-design the classroom and surrounding hall into their vision of what Egypt looked like 5,000 years ago. Students nominated a committee of their peers to organize the exhibition setup, layout, promotion, positioning of students, work to be displayed, and timeline for the event. I told them I would be "waiting in the wings" if needed.

Students hit it out of the park. On exhibition night, two confident student presenters welcomed parents to the museum. They carefully detailed the exhibits on the map and explained how parents could orient themselves. A student mummy awaited them at their first stop—adorned in toilet paper and hidden in a cardboard sarcophagus, he popped out after enough parents filled the room. A wandering "artist" traversed the room to share more around hieroglyphics and Egyptian murals. There was also an Egyptian "makeup station," hand-puppet show, and food-making corner. To exit the museum, parents had to board a student-made cart and traverse through each stage of the "afterlife." A cute sixth-grade girl dressed as Anubis was there to guide them through the process. Student-designed murals depicted each stage.

Most importantly, every student had agency in what they shared and how they built it.

My ego was brought back to earth, and faith in student-centered environments restored. They did infinitesimally better than I could ever have if curating the museum on my own.

How might you involve students in the process of work/exhibition curation? Students might assist with finding an audience; creating invitations; organizing the event program; providing feedback on student booths; or getting permission from admin to book a space. Whatever way you decide to involve students, *I promise* it will yield greater returns than if you do it on your own. Most importantly, it will help you feel more confident in becoming a facilitator of learning.

Virtual Exhibitions and Reaching Global Audiences

When COVID shut schools down and moved the entire educational landscape into an online space, many teachers abandoned the idea of a public audience for student work. Who could blame them? There was no handbook for how to engage students in an online environment the same way we did in a classroom. Most of us were barely trying to keep our heads above water. Yet while the medium for learning might have changed, the underlying factors motivating student output did not. Work needed to be meaningful, connected to a student's individual interests, and shareable with an audience beyond their teacher.

Most importantly, learners needed to be included in the conversation of what that might look like.

Alison Yang, a brilliant Middle Years Programme (MYP) Coordinator and student-centered practitioner included her students in that conversation during the height of COVID in May 2022. Shouldering the responsibility of coordinating more than 100 student personal projects, she faced a dilemma.

Should they put personal projects on hold or continue them in an online space? After bringing the dilemma to her learners, although there was understanable trepidation, one thing was abundantly clear: They did not want to put their projects on hold.

And in the same way she would in the classroom, Alison organized student committees to support peer project development, and the exhibition of their work in an online space. Using a program called "Gather Town" (https://www.gather.town/) the committee helped set up virtual exhibition spaces, an online map for how to navigate, protocols for how to present, and outreach correspondences to gather a global audience.

The exhibition was stunning. More than 50 students presented in a shared virtual space. I attended one virtual booth to watch a student perform magic tricks, and share his journey in becoming a young magician; another student played a song and discussed her journey in becoming a composer; and another student shared sketches/illustrations and discussed his journey of becoming a cartoonist and game designer. Even more impressive than their final work products was the way they articulated their journey. That was also intentional. Here's Alison:

> Very often in an exhibition, we see a final product. We say, oh, that's amazing. You made a guitar, that's amazing. You wrote a song, that's amazing. A lot of times people don't see what's underpinning. The process before they

get to that finishing point. They don't see they fail and then continue to struggle to meet due dates. So I really want to use that exhibition as an opportunity to celebrate their perseverance and resilience.

Get the full writeup from Alison herself here: https://alisonyang. com/8-steps-to-organize-a-virtual-exhibition-via-gather-town/

While most of us have returned to face-to-face learning for some time now, I wonder how you might still use the online space to reach wider audiences for your students' work?

VIS Better Lab School in Taipei hosts a student-led radio station on YouTube to share its take on local topics from a youth perspective.

Seaview Learning in Massachusetts hosts an Instagram and Facebook page for students to share their work on projects ranging from sustainable building to water testing and purification of their local pond.

McCall Elementary School in Waukegan, Illinois, hosts school-wide virtual exhibitions around nationwide events like Black History Month through Google Meets.

When the Audience *Is* the Beneficiary

Curating audiences for student work is even more impactful when the audience for student work *is* the beneficiary. This was the case when a secondary teacher at an international school in Thailand got creative with his geography standards. With summer vacation only a few months away, he tasked his upper elementary students with developing potential travel itineraries for their parents. They mapped out routes, put together sample itineraries, developed options for varying budgets, organized historical information, and even learned some of the language of each potential country their family might visit. They organized the options in a cohesive website and presented the options to their parents just in time to take advantage of low fares.

Static geography and history standards were instantaneously given new life.

Some students planned historical trips to the ruins of East Asia, including Angkor Wats and the Great Wall of China, while other students planned train trips to the major landmarks of Europe, including the Eiffel Tower and the Colosseum in Rome.

This is the kind of learning that student-centered practitioner Alexa Lepp describes as moving "past the teacher's desk and out into the community." It's the kind of learning that doesn't require artificial incentives like grades or awards, but real stakes that benefit a multitude of people.

As Rosie Westall (our democratic-based teacher from Chapter 2) mentioned, "It's amazing what happens when we start saying *yes* to our kids."

One of my most life-changing student-centered experiences occurred because I said "yes" to a shaggy haired sixth-grader 15 years ago. Knowing the whole school had a week off the time-table in March, he proposed an idea that initially terrified me. "Mr. Wagner, for our Intersession Week, can we take a trip to the East Coast?"

I had never taken a trip with a group of students outside of San Diego. I immediately thought of all the planning it would require. We would have to raise money for the trip; plan detailed itineraries; create emergency plans; book accommodations; get parental permission; plan lessons and activities; take into account food allergies. The list goes on. And while I didn't say "no" right away, I was certainly planning on it. I told the excitable sixth-grade boy that I would think about it.

I brought the idea to a colleague of mine who taught math/science across the hall. His response was seven of the most memorable words I heard as an educator: "Why not have the kids plan it?"

Brilliant.

I told the eager, shaggy-haired boy that I would consider his idea for the trip only after he presented a proposal that answered the following questions:

Where would we go? What would be our rough itinerary?
How much would the trip cost? How would we fund the trip?
What would we learn? How would we learn it?
How many students would we take?

How would we get parental permission?

How many chaperones would we need? What would their responsibilities be?

In less than three days' time, he had the answers to all of those questions. He also gathered 15 students who hoped to embark on the journey with him. That trip to the East Coast paved the way for an international trip to China the very next year. It also began a 15-year love affair with this region of the world. Here I am now, residing in a top floor apartment less than 50 kilometers away from where we landed .

It's incredible what happens when we say "yes" to kids.

And students will work harder for you than they ever have before when the beneficiaries are the audience for their work.

What audiences might you have students work for?

Students can enhance their language skills by developing English resources for the students at the foreign language school across the street.

Enhance their storytelling techniques by developing memoirs for the elderly home three blocks away.

Improve their understanding of sustainability by developing Green measures for the non-profit next door.

These are *all* real learning experiences run by student-centered practitioners no smarter or more creative than you are.

Secret tip: You don't have to find these audiences on your own! Task your students with finding audiences and beneficiaries for their work. I witnessed one classroom take their new-found skill of infographic creation and use it to help non-profits piece together their stories. I also witnessed a class undergo a unit on biodiversity protection find non-profits to partner with, both to share ideas and gather additional insights into how the issue was affecting the region.

"Win–Win": Help Corporates "Give Back"

Several corporations have mandates to "give back" to local schools in the region. But most have no idea where to start. Your classroom can make the job easier for them by making the initial contact. One of my middle-school classrooms connected to a local furniture design company called SteelCase to help inspire possibilities for classroom redesign. We took a field trip to their company headquarters to test out various chairs, desks, seating configurations, and space design before small student teams proposed their own. SteelCase was able to do more than simply tick its "community outreach" box on annual reports. It gained a new client in our school, as well as new ideas for how it expanded operations into the school setting!

What potential corporate partners exist within walking distance from your classroom/school?

Betsy Orenos, High School Innovations Teacher and Instructional Coach at Colegio Decroly in Guatemala, helped high school physics students partner with the local amusement park. In small teams, students developed possible ride designs in Virtual Co-spaces and then shared them in a virtual presentation. Imagine the excitement your students would feel if during summer vacation they took their family on a ride they helped design!

Students as Teachers: The Easiest Way to Build Public Audiences for Work

I know what you might be thinking.

Your plate is already overflowing with day-to-day tasks as an educator. How are you supposed to find time to build community audiences for your students' work?

The good news is that some of the most authentic audiences exist within our school's walls. What is a current concept, unit, project, or set of lessons that you have to teach? What would happen if you tasked your students with finding a way to teach it to peers?

This is what innovative educators at Marian Baker School in Costa Rica did with its coding and Sustainable Development Goals (SDG) curriculum. Rather than spend hours of time lecturing students on each sustainable development goal from the front of the classroom, they allowed small teams to research and create games to teach each SDG goal to their peers. Older students transformed their classroom into a miniature arcade, with each game teaching key sustainability concepts. Imagine watching an eight-year-old navigate the underwater world to collect as much waste as possible while learning about its origin, effect on biodiversity, and how to minimize it.

Math educators at American International School Hong Kong took a similar approach with their STEM curriculum. Rather than teach Newtonian physics or algebra using teacher-designed demonstrations or problems from a textbook, teachers tasked high school students with designing self-contained STEM kits to teach these concepts to peers.

In student-centered environments, everyone is a teacher.

Year 12 and 13 English students at Cambridge International School in Slovakia transformed into teachers when studying A-Level Grammar and Text Analysis in the fall. Dry and uninspiring grammar rules like parallel structure, pronoun-antecedent agreement, modifier placement, and subject-verb agreement were given new life when taught via student-generated brain pop videos, comic strips, and colorful infographics. Imagine the excitement 12-year-olds felt when learning from teahers only four years older?

There's data that suggests that learners benefit in several new ways when learning from peers. In an Introduction to Teaching course in Agricultural Education, researchers found that when students engaged in peer teaching activities, they improved metacognition, self-reflection, and overall engagement in the learning process. Peer-to-peer teaching can also improve academic performance. In a peer-assisted learning course for medical school students, those who participated obtained higher scores at several intervals when compared to their non–Peer Assisted Learning (PAL) peers. In addition to academic aptitude, peer assisted learning also improved physical competencies, teamwork and leadership skills, lifelong learning attributes, and comfort with uncertainty.

But transforming your students into teachers benefits more than just your students. It also frees up your time to facilitate the learning process.

Imagine if rather than spend hours of precious time at the beginning of each year searching and curating resources across the Web to better engage students, you had a repository of student-generated materials already at your disposal. You will be gifted with free, engaging learning resources for years to come!

What teaching material do you have that needs a fresh perspective? Which are your most dreaded standards? How might tasking students with creating teaching resources around this material bring it new life? Who might be a potential beneficiary/audience of their work?

We've talked a lot about finding public audiences for student work.

Not all of us are fortunate enough to be at a place like High Tech High or the Creative School of Hong Kong that exhibits student work for public audiences on a regular basis; or at schools that have a full-time outreach coordinator to find those audiences for us. But *all* of us are part of learning ecosystems that aren't far outside our classroom walls.

As student-centered practitioners, it's our job to find creative ways to connect to them. It could be as simple as inviting another class in to view our students' work or offer feedback during its creation. It could be as simple as partnering with another classroom to explore a big topic, or to answer a big question. Expanding the audience for our students' work will empower and engage them in ways that are impossible to achieve if we are their only audience. They will become more reflective, discerning, collaborative, and committed to the learning process.

In the next chapter we move beyond short-lived public audiences, and into the development of long-term sustainable partnerships within our community.

Shift #11: Audience for Work

Teacher < --- >Authentic, public audience					
	1	2	3	4	Now	Next
	Seedling (Sower)	Budding (Builder)	Blossoming (Beacon)	Flourishing (Facilitator)		
Audience for Work	Audience for student work is the teacher.	Audience for student work is the class or other members of the school community but is not authentic and has little relevance to learning experience goals/outcomes. Students have little to no choice who, when, and where to exhibit their work.	Audience for student work is a relevant public audience with student input on who, when, how and where students exhibit their work; but is not regularly involved and limited in scope.	An authentic, public audience is used for exhibition of student work, and during numerous stages throughout learning experiences. Students help find these audiences and plan showcases on their own with gentle guidance from the Facilitator.		

Reflective Questions

1. Pick a learning experience, unit, set of lessons, or project. Who might be a potential audience for your students' work?
2. What is the best way to exhibit this work? (Think event, gallery, presentation, digital space, etc.)
3. How might you make the exhibition of student work more visible within your own classroom?
4. What other classroom, teacher or colleague might you partner with to extend learning beyond your four walls?

SILOED, CLASSROOM BASED

**LEARNING
IS ONE WAY**

MULTIPLE D

**TEACHER AUDIENCE
FOR WORK**

**ONLY ONE METHOD FOR
SHARING**

PLATFORMS FO

**LEARNING CONFINED
BY SCHOOL WALLS**

**WORK HAS
LIMITED IMPACT**

IMAGE 11.3 Shift 11 Authentic, Community-Connected Learning Infographic

AUTHENTIC, COMMUNITY CONNECTED

AL & PHYSICAL

WORK HAS CLEAR IMPACT IN COMMUNITY

STUDENT CURATED PUBLIC EXHIBITIONS OF WORK

COMMUNITY PARTNERS

SENTATIONS/SHARING

LEARNING EXTENDS INTO THE COMMUNITY (MAPPING, FIELD TRIPS, EXCURSIONS, INVESTIGATION, ETC.)

CO-CURATED LEARNING WITH COMMUNITY FEEDBACK (DATA COLLECTION, FEEDBACK ON IDEAS, WORK SAMPLES, ETC)

@kwagssd3

TRANSFORM
EDUCATIONAL CONSULTING

Bibliography

Avonts, Marijke, et al. "Does Peer Teaching Improve Academic Results and Competencies during Medical School? A Mixed Methods Study - BMC Medical Education." *BioMed Central*, BioMed Central, 4 June 2022, bmcmededuc.biomedcentral.com/articles/10.1186/s12909-022-03507-3

"Cospaces Edu for Kid-Friendly 3D Creation and Coding." *CoSpaces Edu for Kid-Friendly 3D Creation and Coding*, www.cospaces.io/. Accessed 14 Oct. 2023.

"Education Resources Information Center." *ERIC*, eric.ed.gov/. Accessed 14 Oct. 2023.

12

Shift #12: From School-Based Beneficiary to Community Partner

IMAGE 12.1 Shift 12 Community-Connected Learning Experiences

> I think the constant level of press and challenge to move the project forward and put out a quality product and keep at it was different for them ... it was real, not just a school task. Knowing they can email an NGO or write to a politician ... they can use their voice to effect change.
> —Dr. Mary Beth Cunat, Principal at Spectrum Progressive School and Global Citizenship Student Ambassador Coordinator

Before we discuss our next shift, I am hoping you will indulge me in a five-minute exercise.

All you will need is a blank white piece of paper, some colored markers, and an active imagination. Begin by writing the

DOI: 10.4324/9781003398226-17

name of a current topic, unit, project, concept, program, or learning experience you normally undergo at the top of the paper. Next, take a colored marker and draw a small circle in the middle of the page. Next, take a different colored marker and draw a bigger circle to enclose that circle. Finally, draw an even larger circle that encloses both circles in a new color. You should now have three concentric circles that fill a majority of the page. The last step is to label each circle. Label the smallest circle, 'School Connections'; the second largest, 'Community Connections;' and the third largest, 'Global Connections.'

You are now ready to imagine.

Close your eyes and envision students forging connections around the topic/unit or learning experience you wrote at the top of the paper …

With different divisions, year levels, and departments at school to conduct surveys and interviews around the topic.

With non-profits, businesses, and government officials in the community to better understand how that topic manifests itself on a local level.

And finally, with other schools, governing bodies, and multinational organizations around the world to affect global advocacy and change.

This is what learning looks like when it extends beyond the classroom.

In the last chapter we discussed the impact learning experiences can have when expanding audiences for student work. But what kind of impact might learning have when school, community, and world are intricately connected to address shared goals through carefully crafted partnerships?

These kinds of partnerships are being forged by learner-centered practitioners just like you. As we discuss each partnership, begin filling your circles with partnerships you might forge within your context.

Our first story begins within a small, progressive school in Rockford, Illinois. Student-centered practitioner and school principal Beth Cunat wondered what might happen when providing students the time, space, and framework to act as citizen ambassadors. Partnering with Meg Languages, she launched an ambassador program for students to ideate, develop, and work on projects that made a difference in their local and global community. Five enthusiastic citizen ambassadors signed up and spent the first session deciding on a topic they found personally meaningful. Given their shared love for animals and the ongoing threats to their habitats, they chose endangered species as their primary focus area. With Beth's guidance, they developed a shared goal-raise awareness and incite a change in the human behavior that led to habitat loss, pollution, and urban encroachment.

First, they populated the School Community circle. Through posters, a website, and a captivating slideshow, they shared their project's aim with the school community and how others could join. They also kept the school community regularly updated on the project's progress via weekly newsletters, parent emails, and at-school assemblies. Before long, the ambassador program had tripled in size.

But they didn't stop there. To help populate the Local Community circle, the ambassadors generated a three-page press release to share their progress and outlined a Digital Stuffy Campaign for other animal enthusiasts to sponsor an animal in exchange for a digital hand-drawn replica. Local media outlets picked up the story and featured the ambassador group on the front page of the local paper!

But the story doesn't end there either. To help make a global impact, the ambassadors partnered with worldwide organizations including World Wildlife Fund and the National Wildlife Foundation, as well as local animal protection groups like Shedd Aquarium and Summerfield Farm and Zoo to attract new memberships and raise funds. Students also sent letters and emailed relevant local, national, and global politicians to introduce and sponsor laws that protected endangered species.

As successful as the project was in enlarging the impact of student work, it was even more successful in enlarging what students previously believed possible.

"No one is too young to change the world. This is the most important thing I have done." —Kenneth, Student Ambassador

"We care about animals. We want the whole world to care about animals." —Julia, Student Ambassador

You might be wondering what Program Coordinator and Student-Centered Practitioner Dr. Mary Beth's role was in the project. Her role was to facilitate the process of forging community connections through asking key questions.

Which animals should we work to protect? What current organizations already support them? Are there existing policies/laws to protect them? Who writes those laws? What's the process of creating them? How do we rally others around our cause? What's the best way to inform our community?

Mary empowered her learners in the same way as Linda Amici and Rosie Hawes did in our chapters around student-led inquiry. Through her careful questioning, students expanded what they believed was possible:

> The constant level of press and challenge to move the project forward and put out a quality product and keep at it was different for them … it was real, not just a school task. Knowing they can email an NGO or write to a politician … they can use their voice to effect change.

How might you expand what your students believe is possible?

You don't have to populate your community circles from scratch. Several organizations outside of school have already created competitions, challenges, and programs to connect your classroom to a broader community.

The "Future City" Annual Competition (futurecity.org/) connects classrooms on a local, national, and global level to design future cities around key challenges and constraints. In some years the challenge is around accessibility; while in others, it's around creating zero waste. Students connect to peers in the iterative process, to mentors in the development of their ideas, and to city planners/urban architects to pitch their cities during the two-day competition.

Model United Nations Forums help connect classrooms across multiple countries to develop resolutions as global ambassadors. In some years, students work together to help decrease nuclear proliferation; while in others, they act together to develop initiatives that lower their respective country's carbon footprint. In the process, students connect more integrally to decision-making procedures, to similar age peers for cultural and language exchange, and to broader global goals.

In Australia, the Dark Sky Competition brings together primary and secondary students to present design solutions around minimizing light pollution. This is a real partnership between schools across Australia and the New South Wales Department of Planning and Industry to help astronomers better observe the night sky. Kelly Pfeifer, the student-centered practitioner who was pivotal in forging the connections, had this to say:

> It's the first time two government departments have ever collaborated together on a project like this. It's also the first time many secondary subjects worked together so collaboratively, including art, English, Hisi (Humanities) and Science. It wasn't just an experience for the enrichment classes, but for all learners.

Imagine the connections and impact your students might make when connecting to global challenges such as these.

With the emergence of dynamic virtual platforms and communities, your students don't even need to leave school to enlarge their impact.

The Global Issues Network (globalissuesnetwork.org) provides a space for students to share their local, sustainable project-based initiatives with a global audience. In hybrid conferences, students share short presentations detailing their project initiative, process, product, and how peers can enact similar projects in their context.

And it's not just large global organizations like GIN (Global Issues Network) that provide this platform. During COVID, student-centered practitioners organized grassroots virtual hubs and gatherings for young changemakers to participate in design challenges around the sustainable development goals. German edu-innovator Till Jaspert developed the Youth ChangeMaker (YCM) Challenge (ycmchallenge.org) to help youth changemakers from more than 80 countries collaborate on learning design solutions for SDG (Sustainable Development Goal) # 4: Ensuring inclusive and quality education for all. One courageous group of young innovators in Afghanistan developed an app and instructional videos to help teach coding to socioeconomically disadvantaged girls.

As a student-centered practitioner, I wonder what regional or global competition/challenge you might connect students with?

How might connecting your students in this way broaden their perspective and overall impact?

One of the simplest first steps in finding these opportunities is to join global educator communities on Facebook, X (Formerly Twitter), or LinkedIn. Some of my favorite Facebook educator groups include The Global Educator Collective, Co-Spaces Edu Community, and ISA Project for Global Education. Within these groups, members regularly share conferences, symposiums, initiatives, and projects they are seeking to collaborate on. I recently witnessed two student-centered practitioners, one from Kenya and one from Thailand, connect their students around designing clean-water access initiatives. Using the design process, students collaborated on joint ideas ranging from homemade water purifiers to artificial wetlands.

Partnerships before Projects

By now, you probably know that I am a card carrying, project-based learning evangelist. If you gave me a megaphone, I would happily sing its praises from the rooftop of my 26th-floor apartment in Hong Kong.

But there's something that I'm an even bigger fan of.

Partnerships.

Partnerships are far more powerful than projects. Partnerships, unlike many projects, imply mutual long-term benefit and include multiple stakeholders who have a vested interest in the results.

Dr. Jane, a seasoned learning practitioner and director of renowned Revolution School in Philadelphia puts it this way:

> It's less about a project, and more about having the mind-set of thinking of all the cultural and social opportunities that are right outside our door. We don't find projects, we find opportunities.

Let's return to that community circle. What opportunities for partnership exist in your community?

In Jane's context, she partnered students with an organization called Philly Cam, a local broadcast youth media organization that uses TV and radio to represent marginalized voices. She also partnered with Report for America, an organization that pairs young journalists with schools to teach the art of storytelling, and uncover stories in the neighborhood. To bring in the creative arts perspective, she and her students forged a partnership with Mural Arts Philadelphia, a public art organization designed to provide transformative experiences, progressive discourse, and economic stimulus to the city of Philadelphia.

Jane finds partners that, as she states, "speak to the DNA of our students, and align to our mission."

Out of partnerships, projects are born. Students worked with Mural Arts to study and examine the countless murals within their community. Philly Cam helped students make sense of the murals and investigate the stories behind them. They helped them piece together each story and weave them together in a student-produced podcast. At present, when city visitors take walking tours of Philadelphia, they can stand at a mural and hear students narrate the story behind it.

Projects have a start and stop date, but partnerships endure.

After students completed the podcast episodes, they continued working on a weekly basis with local journalist Michael Butler to discover new stories and hone their storytelling skills. They uncovered stories of social justice and plights of local heroes in the Black Lives Matter movement.

For Jane, the P in Project-Based Learning is for more than just Partnerships— for her the P is also about People and Place.

What opportunities exist for connecting with place, people, and partnerships in your context?

Our students are ready to contribute to real people, places, and organizations in their community, but we have to provide them with the landscape. Forging first connections becomes much easier when we have the courage to think outside our immediate sphere.

Julia Kao, former principal and Community Outreach Curator/Coordinator at VIS Better Lab school in Taipei, Taiwan, forges partnerships on a regular basis. She describes herself as a "dot connector," connecting people and places across multiple domains. Working with several community partners, she founded a creative community art exhibition space called Oomph. Oomph hosts monthly workshops, performances, and art exhibitions around a dedicated theme. Imagine dancers, artists, performers, and musicians all sharing their interpretation of the theme of Dreams.

Using the same dot-connecting mindset she used in co-creating Oomph, she helped connect her students with a museum space called Garden 91. Together, they explore several what-ifs.

What if Garden 91 could be a community space for shared learning?

What if our museum could make a social impact?

What if we developed unused space in our museum to bring together people of all backgrounds to share in tending it?

Through their what-ifs, a community project was born. Students partnered with the museum to co-construct community gardens that brought the community together on a regular basis. One student group was in charge of signage; another, deciding on which plants to grow; another, how to fertilize and create ideal soil conditions; another, constructing the planter beds; and another, creating compost. Through the process, not only did they bring together often disparate parts of the community, they also brought together disparate parts of the curriculum, connecting engineering, design, marketing, and environmental science in authentic ways.

Julia shared more around what made the partnership successful:

> If you find community partners, just to check certain boxes that relate to your project, even if they're onboard, it's going to become an obligation or chore because they're not really bought in … I think that when choosing a community partner, it's important to understand the why and be on the same page.

Partnerships before projects.

How might you, as a learner-centered practitioner, find community partners that align to your goals and mission?

You might:

◆ Host a networking night for local non-profits: Invite non-profits in to network with teachers around current initiatives, mission, and where they need help

- ◆ Connect with your parent-teacher association (PTA): Parents often have connections to local businesses, community organizations, or professional networks and can make the introductions
- ◆ Attend local exhibitions and events: Attend community exhibitions and events and meet with the organizers to explore how your classroom or school might get involved
- ◆ Join a MeetUp Group: Join a community MeetUp group related to curricular, personal, or student interest and forge new relationships
- ◆ Connect with cultural institutions: Museums, art galleries, theaters, and libraries often have workshops and artist-in-residence programs that can easily be integrated into long term learning experiences or units of study
- ◆ Collaborate with grad school departments at local universities: Master's and PhD students are always in need of community partners for their research projects. Find areas of overlap with your own class/subject's objectives

Remember, when approaching potential community partners, it's important to explore shared goals. Within these goals, where is there an opportunity for mutual benefit and overlap? In Dr. Jane's case, students benefited from professional expertise and equipment to hone their public speaking, storytelling and art skills, while the partnering organizations benefited from student-curated media to enlarge their impact. In Julia's case, her students benefited from a space to build, tinker, and develop a deeper connection with the land; while the partnering organization benefited from increased visitors and visibility.

From Global to Local: Using the Sustainable Development Goals as a Starting Point for Partnerships

We spoke around the importance of starting partnerships by exploring and aligning on common goals. And while an exploratory conversation is helpful in developing long- term relationships, because of limited time, sometimes we need a more targeted starting point.

The 17 Sustainable Development Goals (SDGs) are perfect for that.

Several businesses, government organizations, non-profits, and schools are not only familiar with these goals but seek to integrate them in the core ethos of what they do.

How might you align on the SDGs most relevant to their work?

This is the approach learner-centered practitioner Meghan Robertson of American International School took when seeking community partners for their experiential, service learning week.

The school partnered with local non-profit Rooftop Republic to address SDG 3 and 12, Health and Well-Being and Responsible Consumption and Production. Rooftop Republic helped students build planter boxes to grow edible plants for the school cafeteria.

The school partnered with local non-profit Africa Centre to tackle SDG 10, Reduced Inequalities. Together, they co-organized events to bring awareness around equity issues and the plight of refugees in Hong Kong.

The school partnered with Voltra and World Wildlife Fund to address SDG 15, protecting "life on land." Voltra taught students ways to preserve Hong Kong's natural environment and worked with students to construct aquaponics systems.

How might you use the SDGs as a starting point for partnerships in your context?

You could display them at your next department or grade-level meeting and find areas of overlap within your mandated topics, standards, and benchmarks, or to spark a conversation with a teacher outside of your subject area around how your subjects might combine to tackle them. Or perhaps as the impetus for a joint community map; mapping out key organizations and landmarks relevant to each sustainable goal.

As student-centered practitioners, SDGS can help us break free from our silos.

That's exactly what the Bangkok Patana School in Thailand is orchestrating with its new citizenship program. Using the SDGs as a framework, teachers and students will leave subject-specific silos to develop and implement interdisciplinary projects that build more sustainable communities; preserve minority cultures; and expand access to learning resources. Science and art will team together to address SDG 14, Life below Water; computing and design technology will team to address SDG 12, Responsible Consumption and Production; mathematics and physical education will team to address SDG 3, Good Health and Well-Being. In addressing these SDGs, it won't just be the silo of the classroom they are leaving; they will also leave the silo of the school. They will partner with an unbounded community of businesses, coordinators, non-profits, and local experts to bring each initiative and project goal to life.

At the end of their three-year journey in the program, students will have had the opportunity to make an impact on all 17 sustainable goals through real, community-based learning experiences.

How might the Sustainable Develpoment Goals help you break free from your silo and partner meaningfullly with the community?

Partnering with Alumni

Our alumni are one of the most untapped sources for partnership. They would love nothing more than to give back to the school/classroom that helped ignite their passion. Giving back could be as simple as connecting over a few Zoom calls or quick visits, and as involved as connecting regularly on a long-term project or initiative.

This is the approach Marymount Secondary School of Hong Kong has taken to partner current students with alumni for its Girls Leadership Program. As some hold leadership roles in prominent non-profit organizations working to address social, economic, and environmental challenges in Hong Kong, they are always in desperate need of additional human resources. Secondary school girls are helping fill that gap.

During a carefully curated networking event, alumni first pitched their non-profit's mission, goals, and current projects, and teams of girls used their unique talents to find ways to assist. From developing social media campaigns for inclusive coffee shops, to building games to help protect local horseshoe crab populations, students are spending dedicated time each week on projects that help advance the non-profit's cause.

Which alumni businesses or organizations might you partner with? How might you partner your students with them to realize shared goals?

You might begin with a simple spreadsheet. You could list all alumni on the left side, and track their current work, roles, special talents, and contact information across the top. When designing a new learning experience, unit, or topic of study, you can pull up the spreadsheet to determine which alumni might be worthwhile to partner with.

You might also try a career fair as a starting point for alumni partnerships and connections. Invite them to host short sessions detailing their current jobs, and field questions from students around their day-to-day tasks. In addition to helping students discover new career possibilities, it is also a soft start for more long-term, sustainable partnerships. I witnessed one student-centered school use this approach to build a connection with an alumnus who now works for NASA. Guess who they connected with over Zoom to excite students around their Space Exploration Unit?

The Impact of Community Partners on Student Learning

I would be lying to you if I told you that building and sustaining community partnerships doesn't take time. As educators, we know time is our most valuable and scarce resource.

And with all the tasks we are asked to perform on a daily basis, from lesson planning to grading to parent emails to 1:1 conferences to differentiating lessons, you might be wondering if it's worth the time forging school, community, and globally based partners to enrich our learning experiences.

I can only speak from my experience, and from the insights of conversations I have had with student-centered practitioners and students just like you worldwide.

It absolutely is.

Here are some insights from students that might help weigh in:

I couldn't believe the amount of messages we ended up getting after we painted the mural. People that didn't even attend our school would send messages [to add to it]. We had more messages than we had space. I didn't think we could reach that many people. I learned not to be afraid to reach out for help!

—Emma, high school student in describing the impact of a Body Positivity Mural she created with school and community partners in Medford, Massachusetts.

"The most powerful part of this project was getting to interview immigrants and learning their backstory of how they got here."

—Shem, sixth-grade student describing the benefit of connecting with immigrants in a Community Faces Project at ISAAC in New London, Connecticut.

"We can change the world by taking on these topics."

—Madison, sixth-grade student describing how she felt after co-developing a website, book, and podcast to share immigrant stories in New London, Connecticut.

"No one is too young to change the world!"

—Kenneth, elementary student describing the empowerment he felt in the Empathy for Endangered Animals Ambassador Project.

Returning to the Circle

Let's return to the concentric circles I introduced at the start of the chapter. By this point, I am hoping you have plenty of ideas to fill them. Start with the community that's most easy to mobilize.

In the school box, consider classrooms, non-teaching staff, colleagues, student clubs, and shared spaces.

Expand to the community. Consider non-profits, museums, galleries, businesses, universities, and governmental bodies that might share similar goals.

Finally, home in on the global box. Consider global issues groups, classrooms in other countries, and global networks.

Below is a quick scorecard to help you target specific areas for growth:

Shift #12: Community Impact

	Classroom Based <------------------------------------->School, Local and Global Community Based					
	1	2	3	4	Now	Next
	Seedling (Sower)	Budding (Builder)	Blossoming (Beacon)	Flourishing (Facilitator)		
Community Impact	Learning experience delivered entirely within the classroom with little to no connection to a wider school, local or global community.	Some community-based experiences including learning trips, expert visits, and design work, but very little connection to student individual project work and to support deeper understanding.	Regular community-based experiences relevant to the overall learning experience including learning trips, expert visits, and design work, with some connection to student individual project work and to support deeper understanding.	Learning experience has a clear community impact that extends beyond the classroom. Community experts, beneficiaries, experiential learning trips, parents, global connections, platforms, and systems are used to make experiences more meaningful and relevant, and to improve overall student work quality and *impact* on the community.		

Reflective Questions

1. What opportunities for partnership exist within your community? To businesses, non-profits, government institutions, and other organizations?
2. How might you connect with them?
3. How might you broaden the impact of a current learning experience or unit of study?
4. What digital communities exist? How might you connect and partner with them?

SILOED, CLASSROOM BASED

LEARNING IS ONE WAY

MULTIPLE D

TEACHER AUDIENCE FOR WORK

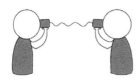

ONLY ONE METHOD FOR SHARING

PLATFORMS FO

LEARNING CONFINED BY SCHOOL WALLS

WORK HAS LIMITED IMPACT

IMAGE 12.2 Shift 11 Authentic, Community-Connected Learning Infographic

AUTHENTIC, COMMUNITY CONNECTED

AL & PHYSICAL

STUDENT CURATED PUBLIC EXHIBITIONS OF WORK

WORK HAS CLEAR IMPACT IN COMMUNITY

SENTATIONS/SHARING

COMMUNITY PARTNERS

LEARNING EXTENDS INTO THE COMMUNITY (MAPPING,FIELD TRIPS, EXCURSIONS, INVESTIGATION,ETC.)

O-CURATED LEARNING WITH OMMUNITY FEEDBACK (DATA LECTION,FEEDBACK ON IDEAS, WORK SAMPLES,ETC)

@kwagssd3

TRANSFORM
EDUCATIONAL CONSULTING

Bibliography

"Future City." *Future City® Competition*, futurecity.org/. 14 June 2023.

Global Issues Network, globalissuesnetwork.org/. Accessed 14 Oct. 2023.

Ycmchallenge.Org - the Springboard for Young Changemakers, www. ycmchallenge.org/. Accessed 14 Oct. 2023.

Part V

Conclusion

In Closing

How do you eat an elephant?

One bite at a time.

Let's return to that blank sheet of paper you started with at the beginning of this book to imagine possibilities. That's the same blank sheet of paper that stared at me when I began my journey to student-centered experiences and environments back at High Tech High. It felt like an elephant. There were so many possibilities, I felt paralyzed.

But when I finally mustered the courage to take that first step, new pathways emerged.

By including students in co-design through regular class meetings and small committees, a new pathway opened to higher quality, authentic student work.

More authentic, high-quality student work opened up pathways for students to reach wider audiences and communities with which to share it.

New audiences for students outside the classroom opened up pathways for deeper connections and partnerships within the community.

Each shift I implemented took a bite out of that massive "teacher-centric" elephant, until pretty soon, my classroom was operating as if I wasn't there. Visitors to my classroom asked the same question I asked that fortuitous day I walked into that learner-centered seventh-grade classroom at High Tech High: "Where is the teacher?"

The same can and will happen for your classroom when homing in on one of the 12 shifts to focus on.

DOI: 10.4324/9781003398226-19

Secondary Teacher Michelle Willis chose the Task Completion Shift: Moving from worksheets, and test-based work to real-world products and services. She worked with students to transition from filling in worksheets and completing disconnected public speaking exercises to creating a collaborative class podcast to feature community stories. The transformation students experienced as a result:

> My students are so much more engaged, enthusiastic, and proud to share their work. As a coach, I am very proud as well.

Elementary teacher Maheen Tiwana built a more student-centered environment by focusing on the Co-design Shift: Moving from Teacher Designed Experiences to Co-designed Experiences by inviting their voice and ideas around how to preserve local animal habitats. When one group asked if they could build an animal sanctuary in MineCraft, the teacher-centered Maheen might have refused, given her limited knowledge of the software, but the new, student-centered Maheen:

> I asked them if it would be possible to make the sanctuaries in Minecraft and also describe the features. They worked impeccably, transferring all of their knowledge into the virtual realm ... These students have long gone to their next class, but I still have regular visits from them telling me about something "cool" they made. Once the students feel "heard," they will talk. Once they talk, you will understand their interests. You learn how to ask the right questions and make students feel like they are the ones directing the project.

A group of secondary teachers at Colegio Decroly in Guatemala decided on the Learning Assessment Shift for their area of focus: Moving from Assessment by the teacher - - - - - -> Ongoing assessment and feedback from students, peers and expert critique. Through self-evaluation, peer feedback forms, and learning journals, assessment became more student-centered. As a result, their principal Emmet Callahan remarks:

We are in the middle of the "end of period" assessments and I can see the difference teachers have made to their assessments. They have the tools and confidence they need to challenge their thinking. Even the veteran teachers have made visible shifts in their practice.

By taking small bites out of a huge, teacher-centered elephant, magic can happen in your classroom as well.

Start with a Question, Not a Goal

What shift (s) will you focus on? How will you go about achieving it?
While this book has provided tips, ideas, strategies, and insights into how to shift to a learner-centered approach, it will be up to you to decide on which ones to explore. View it as an experiment. An inquiry that you and your students can explore together. Rather than limit yourself to a prescribed Goal, open yourself up to new possibilities with a wondrous question.

Make it open-ended, in the same way we ask our learners to engage in learning experiences that have no fixed results. Use the frame, What happens when _____? or What will my classroom look like if _____? or How might we _____?

If you are focusing on the task shift, exploring how to make tasks more collaborative, your question might be: What happens to student collaboration when they co-design the roles, tasks, and frameworks for how they work together?

If your focus is shifting to a public audience for student work, your question might be:

What happens to the quality of student work when students organize exhibitions for younger peer groups?
If your focus is helping students reflect on their learning process as much as they do the product, your question might be: How can we share the story of our learning journey in meaningful ways?

These questions allow for multiple answers and open you up to strategies for how you might go about addressing them.

You've Got a Question: Time to Find a Tribe to Help You Answer It!

Becoming a student-centered practitioner is not easy. It's even more challenging when you try going about it alone.

While we may be part of departments, grade levels, or other school-based teams, few of us have a Tribe of like-minded practitioners equally dedicated to building agency in their classrooms.

Without that Tribe, there's too much temptation to revert to old ways.

It's not surprising self-paced courses have a completion rate hovering somewhere in the ballpark of 5–15 percent, whereas community, cohort-based courses have a completion rate of more than 85 percent. When we find a tribe, not only are we more likely to persevere when things get rough, we also have a like-minded group for regular interaction, feedback, idea sharing, collaboration, and belonging.

Have you found a tribe?

If not, I want to connect you to one. I've now had the pleasure of connecting countless student-centered practitioners to their mastermind tribes. They span all age groups, subjects, learning environments and schools. Here's what one member said who is part of a tribe spanning practitioners from Hong Kong to Middle America:

> Despite what some people may think, finding a learning cohort that you feel comfortable with being vulnerable in, as well as being challenged by, is not easy. However, I have found it in Kyle Wagner's Coaching group. They have opened my eyes to new perspectives and pedagogies, inspiring deep thinking and reflection with every meeting. Not only that, during a time where the world is divided and isolated in so many ways, the cohort has provided a "soft place to land," an opportunity to connect and dialogue with colleagues whose love for teaching transcends race, gender, and political affiliation. Due to the goals formulated within this dynamic group, my experiences in the classroom have broadened, and my desire to incorporate project-based learning into every

facet of instruction has grown from a flame to a wildly raging fire which has ignited my students, the ultimate victors, to shine.

—Brett Carrier, 12 Shifts Cohort Member

Here's from another member of that tribe:

As teachers, we've all had times when we feel unmotivated, when teaching becomes monotonous. Kyle's coaching sessions have helped reignite my passion for teaching, encouraging me to continue to strive for a child-centered classroom. His genuine and meaningful coaching keeps me motivated on my teaching journey.

—Rosie Howes

Here's what the member of a learning tribe in Lahore, Pakistan, had to say about her experience:

Thank *you* for being the kind of facilitator who made every student feel valued and acknowledged in the class. Thank you for making the learning as personalized as you possibly could. Thank you for always encouraging us— even when we came up with the most absurd responses ever! Thank you for being prompt and thoughtful with your feedback. Thank you for making the learning meaningful by adjusting it according to our context. Thank you for your punctuality no matter which part of the world you were in - and always accommodating us by adjusting the classes according to our situation. Thank you for maintaining a friendly, safe and non-judgmental class environment. Thank you for being the kind of modern-day facilitator that we read about in our PD sessions. Thank you for everything!

These are new student-centered practitioners whose classrooms will be forever changed.

With learners who will be newly empowered.

Engaging in learning experiences that allow for voice, choice, inquiry, community connection, and authentic opportunities to make a difference.

All because they got out of their silos and found a tribe.

Want to join us? Learn more and find your student-centered tribe here: www.transformschool.com/12shiftsmasterclass.

This book provided the initial seed; connecting to a tribe will help water and nourish it.

Returning to Our *Why*

Let's return to our Why? Why in a time of increased demands, responsibilities, learning mediums, absenteeism, class sizes, and well-being issues did we stay in a profession that is mostly undervalued by society? Especially when several educators are resigning in droves.

We didn't stay for the summers off.
We probably didn't stay for the accolades.
We certainly didn't stay for the pay.
And we most definitely didn't stay for early retirement.

We stayed because we know there is no other profession in the world where you have the opportunity to make a life-changing impact on young people every day. There is no greater joy than watching the eyes light up in a child who discovered they could do something for the very first time. All because we believed in them.

Thank you for all you do and continue to do for our young people. Serving you is my greatest joy.

Your [co] learning experience designer,

Connect with Kyle
Email: kylewagner@transformschool.com
Website: www.transformschool.com
LinkedIn/Twitter (X): @kwagssd3
Facebook: @transformyourshool

Get the exclusive free resources mentioned in this book for making shifts in your own classroom at www.transformschool.com/12 shiftsbookresources.

Bibliography

"Top Statistics on Cohort Based Learning (2023)." *Learnopoly*, learnopoly. com/cohort-based-learning-statistics/#:~:text=The%20 statistics%20paint%20a%20clear,of%20belonging%20to%20a% 20community, 5 May 2023.

For Product Safety Concerns and Information please contact our EU
representative GPSR@taylorandfrancis.com
Taylor & Francis Verlag GmbH, Kaufingerstraße 24, 80331 München, Germany

www.ingramcontent.com/pod-product-compliance
Ingram Content Group UK Ltd.
Pitfield, Milton Keynes, MK11 3LW, UK
UKHW020931180425
457613UK00012B/311